CW00539663

Dear Mum

Dear Mum

LETTERS FROM ORKNEY TO SHEFFIELD

SUSAN TYZACK

First published in 2023 by Fuzzy Flamingo
Copyright © Susan Tyzack 2023

ISBN: 978-1-7391535-9-5

Editing and design by Fuzzy Flamingo
www.fuzzyflamingo.co.uk

A catalogue for this book is available from the British Library.

For Matthew

Contents

Amongst some of the loose ends to be tidied up after World War One was the Peace Treaty with Turkey, which was signed at Sevres on the 10th of August 1920.

However, this event held little significance in the Walker household on Cemetery Road, Sheffield. The wonderful event there was the birth of the beautiful first and only child of Susannah and Albert Walker, one Lilian Mary who arrived at teatime on that Tuesday afternoon, weighing in at 7½lbs.

From the memoir of Mary Tyzack, nee Walker

21.2.52

How pleased we all were when we heard the good news at 10.30. I have been thinking about you all day and I thank God for bringing you and your dear baby safe through. It is a load off my mind. I hope and trust she will give you and Ron as much pleasure as you have given us. I am longing to see both of you…

Letter from Suey Walker to Mary on the birth of Susan

"In short, said Álvaro, there seem to be two types of people, wouldn't you say? Those who always leave and those who stay put."

Traveller of the Century
Andrés Neumann, Pushkin Press

Prologue

"Mum!" yells my son, and pulls me out of the path of the huge luxury coach. A hiss of brakes and my heart is pounding. Confused, I'm back on the pavement shaking, and a coach driver glares at me. Tired and disorientated, feeling like Inverness was a foreign city, I'd looked left instead of right and stepped out, almost under the wheels of the bus. That would have been a fine start to the holiday. Chastened and subdued, we walked gingerly along a bit of the riverbank and then made our way back to the safety of the railway station.

We'd left home at around 10pm the previous evening, changed at Crewe, and near midnight boarded the Caledonian Sleeper. So excited, in our twin berth, with the complimentary toiletries and the free Penguin Little Black Classics book; I bet they don't give you those any more. I hadn't been on a sleeper since travelling from Mombasa to Nairobi in 1965. The rhythm of the wheels had failed to rock me to sleep, there was shunting and clanging in the wee small hours, hence the exhaustion-induced near accident. But all was well, and we heaved our bicycles on to the next train for the three-hour slog up through The Flow Country, through Caithness to Thurso. In a few hours I'd be hooked, falling in love with Orkney.

In those days, the late nineties, you could take a child anywhere by train for £1 if you had a family railcard. My son Matthew had a map of the railway network on his bedroom wall. We planned our holidays partly by seeing how far we could make that £1 take us, and the station at Thurso in the far north of Scotland was calling us. The Orkney islands were only a short hop over the Pentland Firth, adding to the attraction of a journey north. On top of *that* was the fact that my mother had been stationed during WWII on the isle of Hoy, and the decision was made.

When people ask me what brought me to Orkney that's my usual excuse: falling for the place whilst on holiday, or the tenuous link of Mum's short stay here.

But there's one factor I rarely remember, and *never* mention. Having lost both parents in quick succession (which felt, as Lady Bracknell suggested, like carelessness) I was unmoored. Grief-stricken, the fantasy of a hypothermic ultimate swim sneaked into my head. Without my anchors I could cast myself adrift. Even my nearest and dearest weren't aware of it. It was obviously never a real option; I had a son, remember. But to swim out in the thrillingly tingling icy water, toes numbing, the slow feeling of warmth and euphoria and never having to get out of the water again – well, it was an idea.

There was a pair of ruined cottages for sale, going by the name of Woo on one of the outer isles, the name itself evocative enough. What's more, the property included a stretch of foreshore: cold, north-facing water. A shorter swim would be an easy option on those brighter, upbeat days.

Now I had the money, and more freedom, but the freedom of grief wasn't all it was cracked up to be.

Alternatively, if I survived, my struggle to restore the cottages could be featured in the weekend supplement of a quality newspaper. I'd fit solar panels, a wood-burning stove, live off-grid and have a few hens. Maybe even get a film crew in.

Instead, several years went by. With my inheritance, I bought a different house in Orkney, already restored, rented it out and went to Africa for two years. I fell in love and stayed nearly five.

When I'm in Orkney, I can barely imagine Africa. I love the cleanness here. The bare, spare horizontals. The smooth sweep of hill and loch, open, untrammelled by trees. The cold smell of the air. The shock of a windless day, or the hunch into a near gale, the lean of the walk into it. The hidden hare in the back garden tussocks, the trilling of a curlew. The long view. The ever-mutable arc of the enormous sky.

When I'm in Africa, the very idea of Orkney is impossible. An almost unimaginable concept. In this other place, the trees soar, indecently glorious in rampant furious growth. Bougainvillea brash and brilliant, luxuriant wrapping of everything. Sensuous scents of ylang ylang, frangipani. Irresponsible fertility. It slightly offends me. Claustrophobic, small skies, a patch of sailor's trousers between the tree canopy. My body unfolds in the warmth, unfurls and relaxes. I stand tall, begin to melt. Birds have time to sing, robin chat and bulbul.

I always said I'd not retire in Tanzania; it's not my country.

In Tanzania I'd always be an expat. "Where is your home place, Madam?" they ask, and I don't know. UK: a vague, general answer satisfies them. You'd have to marry an African, I think, forgetting that once I almost did that very thing. But that was in another country and besides…

Though Orkney is not my home place either, it's less alien, even for an incomer, a 'ferry-looper'. The community takes you in and enfolds you, and quickly finds out your business.

The only trouble is, in Orkney I'm old. Another old person.

Not in Africa, I'm not old. In Africa I'm just – I just am.

May 2015

On the beach this evening, four pairs of eider ducks sit on a slab of rock that forms a low platform jutting into the unusually calm sea. There's a whiff of stale seaweed. The males are intent on courting, taking it in turns to throw back their heads and make a low 'woo-ooing' noise: very apt. The females appear to take no notice apart from the occasional adjustment of the lie of their chest feathers. Further back on the sand there are lots of little clear jellies, no more than 2cm across, left behind by the tide. Glittering in the evening sun. These are the so-called 'comb jellies' or ctenophores, which swim using rows – 'combs' – of cilia, and they're decorating the beach in front of one of Orkney's most impressive neolithic sites: Skara Brae.

Yes, I've moved, exchanging Moshi, Arusha, Usa River (*Oosa*), Same (*Sam-may*) and Mwanga in northern Tanzania for the *almost* equally exotic Stromness, Birsay, Quoyloo, Kirbister and last but not least, Twatt. Sometimes pronounced Twot or Twoth with a bit of a lisp. But often, as my friends like to snigger, Twat. Other names on the Ordnance Survey map are even more foreign: Swartland Road that leads to Dounby passes a house called Benzieclett; on the island of Wyre there's the Point of the Wart; there are hills called Quinni Moan,

Tooin o' Rusht, Muckle Billia Field and the Knowes of Trotty. But Twatt is where my house is with its *plantie-creu* – a semi-walled vegetable garden – its front garden of windswept grass and its couple of neglected fields. The house was built from the remains of an old house by Bob and Mymic Fidge when they retired from their farm. Kristin, at the post office, says she's not been in that house for years, not since Bob and Mymie Flett lived there.

"Flett?" I ask.

"Oh yes, Fidge was the name of their farm on the aerodrome." In Orkney, people get called after the place where they live. (Does this mean from now on I have to be called Susan Twatt? Surely not!) To the south, the hills of Hoy are visible on a good day, and to the west the land rises, blocking my view of the sea; a mile and a bit up the hill towards Quoyloo is the Orkney Brewery. West Mainland of Orkney has been described as a saucer shape, the rim of the saucer being the coastal cliffs and the centre of the saucer being the inland freshwater lochs: Boardhouse, Swannay, Hundland and Sabiston, Stenness and Harray. Over to the east, across the central marshy bit, I can see the lights of Dounby at night.

I stand in the kitchen and watch the oystercatchers and lapwings, curlews and hares in the garden. The curlews are courting. The male, wings flicking, stands behind the female, prodding the back of her neck with his crazily long beak. He gets closer and closer until they're touching, still wing-flicking, still sexily tickling her neck. And suddenly I've blinked and it's over – they go their separate ways, shrugging and preening. One morning there are at least eight of them, scuttling, heads down, apparently following each other in circles.

I'd decided, on leaving Tanzania, that a new adventure was in order; Orkney was an appealing alternative to my previous UK abode. If the worst came to the worst – especially concerning the weather – I could always go somewhere else. A spell in Africa, almost five years in a two-roomed house, had worked wonders for my attitude to possessions. The whole process of sorting, selling, recycling, charity-shopping, giving away or as a very last resort tipping stuff was a welcome therapeutic distraction from the trauma of leaving Mwenge University, my beloved students, my job, friends and the warmth and vibrancy of Africa. In the space of a month, with a LOT of help from my friends, the accumulated belongings of several lifetimes had been dramatically reduced and I was ready.

I drove up with my friend Anne, reassuring company and good advice as to the positioning of the furniture. When she left, my son Matthew came from London and rotavated the vegetable plot. Then I was left to my own devices. 'Home' alone.

April in Orkney was lovely; daffodils fringed the roadsides, marsh marigolds lined the ditches. The weather was not too cold, but the wind was biting and the house was chilly because I had not a clue how to light the antiquated once solid fuel but now oil-fired Rayburn. When I did find out how to start it, having 'got a man in', it was too hot and uncontrollable.

At first, the fields were empty – a few sheep in evidence.

Then the lambs appeared, the animals with, as Matthew said, the highest correlation of cuteness to deliciousness. One breed had panda-faced lambs: white all over with black eyes, ears, mouth and knees. Over the next few weeks, the fields fill up. First the black cattle appear in the field next to the old cinema that once provided entertainment for the Royal Air Force base of Skeabrae and is now another barn. No one else sends their cattle out for ages, but by the end of May there are lots; gangly-legged calves look startled at the big wide world. They mill around, calves and mothers alike, as if drunk and delighted by all this sky and grass. There are still not as many cattle as there should be, though. My neighbour, Moira, is complaining about the weather: "It's the farmers I feel sorry for," she says, "they cannae get the kye oot, and they're running oot of food."

Walking along the road is an amazing experience for a pedestrian. The vehicles give one a wide berth. As soon as a car driver spots a walker in the distance, they begin to move out into the opposite lane as if in fear of being ambushed by a stone-wielding maniac who might lob boulders through the windscreen. Or maybe they are taking precautions in case lightweight walkers like me are blown into the path of the vehicle by the force of the wind. It's a refreshing change from Tanzania, where the pedestrian risks life and limb merely by being on the roadside in the first place and is forced to scramble as far as possible into the verge-side vegetation (usually prickly) in order to avoid being mown down. Even then you can feel the draught as the bus or lorry whistles past by a hair's breadth.

One thing that Orkney does have in common with Tanzania is time. There's a saying: "No hurry in Africa"; it seems there is also no hurry in Orkney. Moira and Chockie are my nearest neighbours and like nothing better than a natter; Moira is not too difficult to understand, but with Chockie you have to listen very carefully. It took several weeks for me to realise that his name is actually Jackie but J in Orkney is pronounced so softly, like a *ch*, so 'just' becomes 'chust'. Aye, it wis chust fine. When they and the local farmer and his family come round for a cup of tea and they're talking among themselves, it's almost a foreign language.

And, like in Africa, it takes time to get organised. There's the internet, which of course doesn't work first time round and the BT man has to come. "Oh," he says, "the fault is at the exchange, this number's going to another house altogether, an empty house." Then for over sixties there's the concessionary bus pass, also enabling one to have four free ferry tickets (including an overnight berth on the route to Aberdeen) and free bus travel anywhere in Scotland. There's the Air Discount scheme that gives Islanders 40% off the air fare to Glasgow, Edinburgh, Inverness or… Bergen! And the Islander ticket that gives you cheap ferry travel even if you aren't a pensioner. They make it easy to escape, but most incomers, making up 20% of the population, I'm told, tell you they wouldn't live anywhere else. Only one man, having been here ten years, says he's looking for somewhere warmer, for example, the Azores – but then he'd moved from Tenerife. Hmm. I've moved from Tanzania.

I make a few sorties to try and get to know people. There's a lot of ways to do this. Considering the size of the population (about 22,000), there's a huge choice of activities – from the archaeology society through local history, natural history, several choirs, to an outdoor swimming club, yoga and Zumba. There are play-reading groups, operatic groups and drama groups, lots of live music from the Scottish Chamber Orchestra to Blazin' Fiddles, and The Phoenix Cinema that screens National Theatre live broadcasts, 'fringe' art house films, as well as the standard box-office hits. One of my first outings was on an RSPB walk to see hen harriers sky-dancing – not a good day for it as it was too cold and grey for anyone to feel like sky-dancing. And the hen harriers were miles away! I'm used to seeing fish eagles perched on nearby branches in an African national park! I did get to meet some wellie-clad birdwatchers but given that they were all bundled up in scarves and woolly hats I'll probably never recognise them again.

An evening was spent with the flora section of the Orkney Field Group. We met on an overcast evening, at a rainy beach, the aim being to walk along cliffs to a spot where we could find Early Purple Orchids. The rain slowed to a drip and we did find them, a few scattered and distinctly underwhelming specimens. I did my best to show some enthusiasm, but I've been spoilt. I kept thinking of the Southern Highlands of Tanzania and Kitulo National Park with its forty-odd species of orchids, of which I'd seen at least ten without even trying... but we live with what we've got, and I cheered up when I found some butterwort in flower. These are always a delight, with their violet-like flower suspended delicately above the light green starfish leaves. As for dandelions, the leader of the group told me that the national dandelion expert had been in Orkney the previous week and of the 234 dandelion species that exist in Britain had identified no less than *forty species* in Orkney alone. Amazing; Kitulo has orchids, Orkney has dandelions.

Now in late May, the dandelions are everywhere – fields full of them. Roadside verges light up as they open in the sun, and suddenly everything's bursting into bloom. Daffodils have faded and been replaced by banks of masses of primroses. The primroses are still there, followed by bluebells but now there's thrift, sea campion, scurvy grass and spring squill. For those who know where to look, the tiniest rare purple primrose, *Primula scotica* can be found pressed to the sea-sprayed turf on the cliffs at Yesnaby.

The geese have got goslings and the hares seem to have given birth to teenagers. The hares, luckily, are fond of dandelions. They swallow the flowers but if these are closed up or finished the stalks seem to be equally palatable. The hare nips off the stalk at its base and then chomps its way upwards until every morsel has vanished, giving me a defiant look through the window. Or so it seems.

So far, so good. The air is clean (it would be: it's blown in fresh every day from either Scandinavia or the North West Atlantic), traffic is negligible and crime almost non-existent. The locals leave their doors unlocked, and a knocked wingmirror makes it into the newspaper. All my boxes are unpacked, the house is comfortable and maybe I'll make it large enough to do bed and breakfast. The hardest part so far is not the wind, or the having to make new friends, but the fact of being retired. I do miss work and, although reading, gardening and bits of arty-crafty stuff can keep me nicely entertained, I don't feel *useful*. What a change – to come from a place where my students appreciated me so much and I was doing more than a full-time job to being just another retired person; of course, there are plenty of opportunities for voluntary work, so I'm looking out for the next challenge. Watch this space.

2

Mary Arriving

Wren Tel L.M.Walker
WRNS Quarters
HMS Haybrake
RN Base
Lyness
Orkney
1.9.44

My dearest Mum and all,

I hope by now you have received at least a card or a letter and that you'll know I'm okay and enjoying life as far as possible. At the moment I'm waiting to have my teeth filled – two of them – they certainly don't waste any time here. We all went to have a dental inspection and some of them have to have about six done – I have been more successful, only two.

The trouble about being here is that I scarcely know what to tell you and what to leave out. Even talking about the weather is barred. Anyhow, the censor will cross out anything indiscreet, so I'll do my best.

First of all, I forgot to tell you about a really grand meal we had in Dunfermline – a lovely restaurant – and we had lots and lots of bacon and chips and bread and butter and tea and delicious cakes, all for 1s8d. I think you would like Dunfermline, it seems a really nice little town.

9

Unfortunately, we missed the best part of the country in Scotland because we travelled during the night and the journey as far as Edinburgh was not terribly interesting because we came by the coast way – through Thirsk, Durham, Darlington, Newcastle and Berwick. We seemed to be travelling almost on clifftops and the sea was just below us but unfortunately it rained for a greater part of the way. However, it was fine when we reached Edinburgh and Betty's mother had brought lots of sandwiches and even a pot of tea for us, which we thoroughly enjoyed as we hadn't had anything to drink since we left home. Auntie Ada's cakes were very good and so were our own sandwiches, Mum.

Mum, I do hope you are all okay and not having any worries, please don't worry and do rest, it seems an awful long time to be without any word from you, but I expect I'll be hearing from you on Monday. I have not yet written to everyone but if you'd like to give my address to various people, I shall be glad. When you send my parcel there are a few things I want, Mum – the rug, of course, but not my shoes just yet, and some washing soap and some starch, for the laundry services are limited to a very few articles, and also my pink sponge bag and a tin of Vaseline – I think I shall need some for my hands in the cold weather – also calcium tablets, I don't want to have chilblains. I must go now. I hate the idea of this dentist but there it is.

Lots of love to all,

Mary

PS Am not allowed to put kisses at the bottom, so please take them for granted.

September 1944, and my mum has been sent to Hoy, for what will be the last few months of the war, though they don't know that. It's the first time she's been so far north, so far away from her home in Sheffield. Her training as a wireless telegrapher in the WRNS at HMS Cabbala in Lancashire was the first time she'd lived away from her parents at all, at the age of twenty-four.

It would be a neat juxtaposition if my move here was at the same age. Instead, I'm almost the same age as her mother was at that time: sixty-four.

Meals feature very heavily in her letters home. They must have been pretty short of food in Sheffield.

Obviously, calcium tablets were a well-known preventative measure against chilblains, at least in the Walker family. If only I'd known that when I came to Orkney. For the first time in my life, I had a huge chilblain on one of my toes, itchy and painful.

Wren Tel L.M.Walker 94167
WRNS Quarters
HMS Haybrake
RN Base
Lyness
Orkney
7th Sept.

My dearest Mum and all,

Very many thanks for your lovely letters, it was great to receive them. They only took two days and it was very good to have them and especially to know that everything is okay, you've no idea how glad I was to hear from you. I have heard from no one else and am wondering what has happened to Dorothy Farrow.

Do you remember my saying I could have gone to Grimsby? Well

I couldn't. All the girls who were going there have been split up and one is here and the others are in various parts of Scotland, so you see things all work out for the best, don't they! I'm glad I'm settled here, even though it is such a long way from civilisation.

Many thanks for sending me the parcel – I can't remember anything I want at the moment, love. You can send me the pullover if you are not using it, if you are I will get another. We are preparing for winter here, gumboots, seaboot stockings and oilskins – real old sea salts – apparently the weather where Jo is hasn't been as good as this so I think it's pretty cold generally.

It is a peculiar feeling being on this little island, we feel as though we are in camp all the time. In spite of it being so lonely and isolated and far from home, I think it will be good fun, everyone is very friendly, all being in the same boat, so to speak.

There is very little in the way of entertainment here except dancing, so I have taken it up to a small extent and went to an army one on Monday, Tuesday went to the cinema with a little Scottish sergeant – one of my partners – and again last night with the girls and to a free 'do' today. Have spent about 1/- this week – I can see I shall have a nice little nest egg I hope by Christmas.

The news is great just now, I'm so glad to hear about Lille.[1]
Well, dears, must say goodnight now.
Much love to all of you,
Mary

---

1   Lille had been occupied by Germany until the 4th of September, 1944. During the occupation, the city was incorporated into Belgium under a single occupation authority. On the 2nd of September the liberation of Lille began and was complete by the end of the morning of the 4th of September. Approximately fifty people were killed and 600 wounded during the liberation.

Mum, I'm so glad you have been to the specialist – what you want more than anything is a holiday and lots more to eat. Don't go without meals. When Dad comes back you must go away somewhere.

How nice for you to have the plums! Of course I would miss the Victorias!

By the way – the boats we go in are not small ones, they are the type we used to have little trips in the Channel in peacetime.

3

June 2015

When I say I miss my students, they do keep in touch with me. On my new smartphone I have WhatsApp and they have started a special group called BIOLOGLY ISSUES (sic) in which they can ask each other or their teachers for help. A good idea, in theory, but in practice a mixed blessing. Occasionally they ask sensible questions like, "What is the difference between a reducing and a non-reducing sugar?" which they could easily find in any A level biology textbook. Sometimes they prefer to find obscure images from the internet and ask, "What is this?" – the more horrible and shocking the better. For example, one photo shows a man with what looks like a huge black cushion sitting between his legs. I wait to see what the others make of it before responding. They all think it looks very strange and horrible and then T, the former acting head of biology, pipes up: "It is contended as bio accumulation of onco virus in the cells of erectal muscles."

So now it's time for me to add my two penn'orth: "It's scrotal swelling caused by filariasis, transmitted by mosquitoes."

"Probably, Sue," replies T, but adds: "Some people here yet have misconception in conceptualization of the concept of '*tezi dume'* (which translates as 'male gland'*)* but we need to search scientific facts on it rather than political quoloqial says."

That's cleared that up then. At times it gets more personal, and I have to respond to a question about why a woman sometimes can't *'rich'* (reach) orgasm.

Tanzania isn't the only place with unusual use of English. "The Café" in Stromness has been on the go under various managements since I first visited in 1997. I did learn a new word from them recently. On the door one weekend was a notice as follows: Sorry we are closed due to embrievement. Embrievement? Is this Orcadian for bereavement? It isn't in the Orkney dictionary, but anything is possible.

My most important house improvement task at the Cott is to get the heating sorted out and replace the inadequate old Rayburn conversion with something more efficient and ideally more sustainable. Should I go for a multi-fuel stove with boiler, wood pellet stove, an electric air-to-air system or simply a modern oil boiler? Various heating engineers or plumbers came and gave their advice. I had an Energy Performance Certificate survey and a Green Deal Assessment, and a heat load calculation. I tried to find out about RHI (renewable heat incentive) payments and loans for renewables, trudging through the labyrinth of information on the energy saving trust's website. One accredited installer who'd come recommended seemed a likely bet but was away on holiday. Meanwhile, I thought, let me get a few more quotes, and I mentioned the name of the holidaymaker to one of the quoters.

"Ha," he said, "Mr Plumbduff! (let's call him that for the sake of discretion) – I wouldn't let Mr Plumbduff through the door!" It turns out, according to Mr Heatwell that Mr Plumbduff is not really accredited at all, in fact: "He's not even a plumber, he's just some sort of 'ologist' who saw how much plumbers were charging and thought he'd call himself a plumber. And the last boiler he installed had to be condemned, you shoulda heard the abuse he gave that wifie at Birsay on the phone when she complained about it. They came up from Surrey to inspect it and then disconnected it and said it can't be used *at all*."

So that was that. Maybe I'd had a lucky escape; the proposed wood pellet boiler scheme fizzled out.

Early June and lots more kye are out. The problem of cattle food has even reached the BBC news, with the headline, "Orkney cows stuck inside due to rain," and one Orkney farmer says the effects might be felt for years to come. An early cattle auction has been organised to help out those farmers who have run out of food and can't risk damaging the pasture by putting them out to grass. For me the kye are yet another entertainment as I look out of the kitchen window. Four fields away a group of fawn-coloured ones suddenly decides to head off up to the top of the field. They start off at a saunter and then charge exuberantly the length of the fence. These cows must be the nosiest cattle in the world. You only have to stand by the roadside and cows in the nearby field will come purposefully over to the fence to see what's going on, and then follow as you walk along the road. At one time, I had two lots keeping me company, one on each side of the road.

In the wet meadows and ditches there's lady's smock in bloom and, along the cliffs, the sea pinks bob about, along with the first bird's foot trefoil, sea campion and tormentil. Around the longest day there's a sudden burst of growth, as if everything is using all the daylight to make up for lost time. There are lots of orchids, ragged robin in the marshy parts and a marvellously weird fern called moonwort I've never seen before, discovered on another walk with the flower group. Even my potatoes decide to make a break for it, with the first leaves warily pushing through. Now I know where they are, I can earth them up.

One still, moist afternoon in the garden tending the tatties, I hear a snipe drumming. Hardly a sound, more of a feeling, a magical vibration that sends shivers down my spine. Eventually I spot it, wildly soaring and diving.

On Marwick beach an old Lidl bag came in handy for picking up a few plastic bottles that had been left stranded. Also washed up were two outers from cauliflowers – the leafy parts, I mean – and an apple. These I left, being biodegradable, and carried the rest home to the dustbin, stinking out the car. Whenever I go to put something in the wheelie bin, the starlings are set screeching. The bins are kept in a stone lean-to that used to be a pig shed until the roof blew off; starlings nest in between the stones. They go mad, perching with mouthfuls of grubs on nearby willows until I retreat and they can go and feed their young. Suddenly, one day in mid-June, it all goes quiet and they've fledged. The top of the wheelie bin is a mess of bird poo, as are the cliffs at the RSPB reserve of Marwick Head five miles away. Walking up to the cliffs I can smell the guano and am immediately transported back to my time as warden of Aride Island in Seychelles and the Sooty Tern breeding season.

Here it's fulmars who patrol the clifftops, and guillemots sit wedged together in black rows against the white ledge background, facing inward; the cliff face is not much of a view for them but maybe it's better than having the salty wind in their eyes? Maybe they balance better that way, given the slope of the ledge? The chunkier razorbills aren't as gregarious and creep further into the crannies. There are a few gannets soaring around and, later, from the other side of the curve, I can see a few pairs on the cliffs. It's good to see some young ones with patchy plumage. And two puffins! I'm with a friend and we each spot a puffin, both of them a little confused and out of place, not, apparently, having found each other. One of them turns and wanders into a little rock mini-cave and wanders out again. It checks it out a couple of times and then flies off. A couple of weeks later, I saw them again, having found each other and inhabiting another hole. Fulmars to the right of them, fulmars to the left of them, stuck in the middle, and still looking bewildered.

The kittiwakes make some sort of a shaggy nest and are much more respectably spaced. I wondered what they make the nests with: seaweed? Floating algae? Then, one day, there they were, in a well organised crowd collecting nesting material. At the back of the bay there's a small lagoon with a sandy scrape by the side, edged with dead grass. The kittiwakes were pulling out chunks of it and heroically heading off into the wind, round the corner to the cliffs, ready for a spot of nest furbishment. They always look so smart and clean-cut, and I recently found out why. They like bathing in fresh water. I watched a crowd of them in Marwick Bay, just off where there's a stream frittering across the pebbles into the lagoon (the Choin), dipping their heads in the water, shaking their wings to wash under the arms. In late June, the chicks have hatched, most of them two to a nest, making it all look rather crowded.

The paths around Marwick Head swarm with rabbits. I wonder if they compete with puffins for burrows. In the evening, the rabbits sit gazing out to the west until I get near and they scatter. There are black ones and peachy coloured ones (at a distance mistaken for a ginger cat), as well as your average grey rabbit; no serious predators here to pick off the less camouflaged flamboyant characters.

At home, two oystercatchers have taken up residence on top of the oil tank. They've been hanging around the garden for ages, testing out piles of dead grass as possible nest sites, but still no sign of either eggs or chicks. They poke that hefty beak into the ground, sometimes jamming their face down into the grass almost as far as their eyes, to reach the juiciest and most elusive worms. Suddenly they discovered that the hard green plastic hollow of the top of the oil tank is very comfortable, and settled there, for all the world as though they are sitting on eggs. It's not that the tank is sheltered from the wind, perched on its own stone plinth. Perhaps the raised mouldings provide a bit of protection for the legs and undercarriage when the birds are sitting down. After a while, they stand, shiver, stretch a leg and proceed with a spot of intensive preening and an animated squawk before flying off. Or they stand on one leg, perfectly balanced avian yoga experts, head tucked under wing. When they finally come back to normal consciousness they can sometimes hardly walk, the newly un-tucked leg apparently getting cramp or pins and needles and needing a good stretch. What's going on? Are they youngsters who don't know what to do? Is it a rare example of homosexuality in the oystercatcher world? Or a phantom pregnancy? I learn that oystercatchers are mainly monogamous, faithful to partners and territory, lay between one and four eggs, mostly three, but sometimes 'dump' eggs on other birds, in a similar way to cuckoos. None of this is much use in helping me to know what's going on with the oil-tank pair, but these are certainly two lazy birds; maybe they've dumped their eggs somewhere else and left another bird to do the hatching and feeding. There's a lot of synchronised squawking, staring, preening and sleeping – usually in that order – but no obvious interactions, no obvious mating either. They rub along together, and then one day they're gone.

* * *

One day we had an expedition to the island of Shapinsay, only a thirty-minute ferry trip away. Waiting to board the ferry, I got into conversation with Aidan, a young man on a bicycle who'd just come off a night shift and was going to Shapinsay to see his girlfriend. You've got to keep them happy, he laughed, not quite easily, as though it was a phrase he'd learnt from his older work mates. I didn't *entirely* understand everything Aidan said (that accent again…) but he was working on the bridge of a boat that was something to do with Billia Croo. This is a renewable energy research project to assess wave and tidal energy systems, based on the west coast just north of Stromness. He'd grown up in Evie, a few miles up the coast from Kirkwall, but now, having left school without doing Highers, had a flat in town as it was easier for work. "So, what do you like doing?" I asked, mentally predicting the stereotypical answers – bars, music.

"I love sailing," he said. "I'm out in my boat whenever I can." It turns out he went to Shetland on leaving school, studying some sort of maritime thing and navigation and now, at eighteen years old, has some sort of a 'ticket'. He let slip the fact that he sailed to Norway, alone in his twenty-two-foot boat with a tiny outboard. "My Mum doesn't know I went to Norway," he admitted. "She thought I was just going to Shetland to see my friends." That's bad enough, I thought. "When I got to Shetland, I still had a week's holiday," he said, "so I thought I may as well carry on. 'Course, I didn't have a visa or passport or anything, couldn't go to Bergen or anywhere big. I just went and explored the fiords a bit."

He was waiting for his girlfriend to be ready to go off sailing on another adventure. I'm a bit dubious: does she like sailing?

"Oh yes," he said, "that's how we met; I was teaching on a sailing course she was on."

When we reached Shapinsay, there she was to meet him,

with brilliant magenta hair. And later, there she was again, helping out in her mother's café.

My quest to be useful led me to the office of Voluntary Action Orkney where I scanned through pages of organisations looking for volunteers. The first of my chosen causes to contact me was in the form of another incomer, Dusty Miller of Barony Mill, who needed volunteer guides to show tourists round the meal mill. It's a working, water-driven mill, the only one in the UK – possibly in the whole world – which mills bere (*Hordeum vulgare*), an ancient form of barley. Bere is to barley as spelt is to wheat. Off I went to the mill to be inducted, a process that consisted of me following Dusty around on his tour a couple of times and having earnest advice about how to read my audience. Like everyone I meet in Orkney, Dusty is *very* talkative. Three hours later, I escaped, having purchased a bag of oatmeal. On my next visit to practise the spiel of a tour guide, I met Rae the Real Miller. Rae's father and grandfather were also millers in the winter and ghillies in the summer, but Rae broke from the mould and went off to be a lighthouse keeper for thirty years before coming back to the mill. Wow! I've never met a lighthouse keeper before! He was stationed onshore or offshore on an island. This could be a proper island such as Stroma in the Pentland Firth, or those known in the trade as rock stations, like the exotically named Sule Skerry, or Muckle Flugga, the most northerly point of the British Isles. Rae met his wife Margaret on Muckle Flugga; not actually *on* the rock, but her sister's husband was also based there, and so they met one Christmas at the shore station on Unst in Shetland where the wives and families stay. One day, over a cup of tea and cake at their house, he showed me his photograph album of lighthouses, from Land's End to Duncansby Head, and I was suitably impressed. Now those places are all automatic and unmanned. He was one of the last in the line, and also could be the last of the millers: none of his five daughters are interested in the job, and he's supposed to be retired. So, if anyone's interested, there's a job vacancy for a miller;[2] I can lend you my reading homework: *The Scottish Country Miller 1700-1900*, and *French Millstones: notes on the millstone industry at La Ferté sous Jouarre*. Who'd have thought it?

I quickly got the hang of the tour-guiding on my one day a week from 10am to 5pm. Supposedly I could have an hour off for lunch but in practice this never happened. Some days it was very quiet with few visitors in the morning, so that if a couple arrived at 12.45, just before lunch closing time, I hadn't the heart to turn them away. Most of them are enthralled to see the old machinery, especially since it all still works. There are stories about the origin of the expression "showing one's mettle" and about how the millstones got to the mill from the quarry on the cliffs at Yesnaby. A digression about how in 1755 the quarry workers were saved from drowning by a herdie boy on the cliffs tending sheep; he saw the approaching tidal wave caused by an earthquake off Lisbon and shouted to warn the men to escape. They all escaped but lost most of their tools.

---

2   Later, Historic Scotland were approached to fund a Craft Fellow. Ali Harcus was trained by Rae and is now the Barony Mill miller. Sadly, Rae died in 2018.

There's a French millstone from a world-renowned quarry just outside Paris,[3] which is so hard that the original one put in when the mill opened in 1873 is still in use, and it was second-hand then. And there is always a magical moment when the visitor releases the lever to allow water over the millwheel. The sound of the water flow changes, there's a suspenseful minute until there's enough power to move the overshot wheel and with a great 'clunk' the gears and stones are in motion.

Bere used to be a vital part of the diet in Orkney and other parts of the north of Scotland, but its cultivation declined with the advent of modern barley, increased oat cultivation and imported wheat. It really is ancient and one of the earliest grains to be domesticated, some grain even having been found in the chambered tombs of Orkney, which date from circa 2500 BC. And it's ideal for the climate here, needing only a short growing season and able to do well on relatively poor soils. It has little need for added nitrogen, unlike the modern barley grown for animal feed and brewing. To look at, it's messy and very hairy; modern barley has two neat rows of grain, but bere has between four and six rows, which makes for lots of awns. Orcadian farmers tell of the itchiness of working with bere, or having the awny stalks poked down their jumpers in mischief by a friend while harvesting in the old days.

Apart from a few experimental plots at the Orkney College Agronomy Institute, it's only grown in a few fields around the mill and the ground beremeal is used by local bakers to make bannocks, biscuits and cakes.

---

3   La Ferté sous Jouarre

I practised using it in different recipes: flapjack, ginger biscuits, rye and beremeal scones and fruitcake, with varying success. The bannocks, a traditional round flatbread, were a disaster, but the others were pretty good. Beremeal adds dark colour and a distinctive nutty flavour. As it is low in saturated fat, low in gluten and has other dietary advantages, we are expecting a surge in popularity, especially with current enthusiasm for ancient grains such as spelt. Better get planting more!

4

Mary's Early Memoir

In those far off days of 1920, the midwife invariably stayed with the family for at least a week before and probably two or three weeks after the baby was born. The good lady concerned in this case was Mrs Booth who lived in Dronfield and was recommended by our local GP Dr Beardmore. From all accounts, she was a treasure and cooked the patient's meals, saw to the baby's washing and was an excellent counsellor and friend as well as an excellent nurse.

My grandmother – my father's mother – lived with us (in Sheffield) and she heartily disapproved of having a "woman in to do" for me, Mother having been brought up in a big family where a woman had to fend for herself and struggled as best she could through umpteen childbirths.

My mother Suey was forty-two when I was born and had been very apprehensive; she later told me that the day prior to my entrance into the world she had been told by the midwife to go for a nice walk and she did. She went up the road and wandered around the General Cemetery full of foreboding as she read some of the inscriptions on the tombstones. However, all was well, and I don't think my arrival was too much of a problem.

Like most babies of that era, I slept in a clothes basket until my parents bought me a very superior – for those days – cot from Redgates.[4]

---

4   The 1920s cross between Mothercare and Toys'R'us

This had a drop side of brightly coloured pictures of nursery rhyme characters on the ends and was so big it lasted until I was at least five years old.

I'm sure I must have been very happy in those early years. My mother had two unmarried sisters, Maggie and Annie, and a brother Bill who lived with their mother, my Granny Wilkinson, in Clun Road at Pitsmoor, a suburb far more upmarket then than it is today. I spent a lot of time at Clun Road, my aunts thoroughly spoiling me. Annie was the dressmaker who worked at home, but Maggie was the motherly, cuddly one whom I came to care for almost more than my own mother. She had been a children's nanny at one time and told me stories of her adventures when they went to their holiday house at Sutton-on-Sea, which sounded to me like a heavenly spot. Uncle Bill was everyone's idea of a favourite uncle and took me to the park, to the pantomime and bought me the first sweets I ever remember.

We lived "over the shop" – my dad had the little boot repairer's shop, which had been his father's, just below the Vestry Hall[5] on Cemetery Road. I won't call him a cobbler because my mother was most offended if people referred to him as a cobbler, however everybody did so in those days. He was a very mild, thoughtful man who never lost his temper and never raised his voice in anger. I think Mother would have appreciated it sometimes if he did, for she liked an argument, but it was peace at any price with Dad.

We had a living room with a Yorkshire range and a small kitchen downstairs. The room over the shop was the drawing room, or lounge, or whatever you like to call it, where we took any visitor. There was a green velvet settee, two armchairs and a bookcase and we had a

---

5   Now, in 2016, a Somali Community Centre. Albert Walker's boot repair shop was knocked down to make way for a supermarket.

Mary's father Albert and his dad James in front of the family shop

Sunbeam gas fire, which was very cosy. We always went up there in the winter if we had been out and the coal fire had gone out. It was lovely to be able to light the fire for instant warmth. We had two attics – one was

Grandma's (Walker's) bedroom and the other was used for general storage like all attics and for drying clothes on wet days.

No bathroom or inside toilet, of course. Indeed, we had to share a toilet with another family in the yard. The Naylors had two boys, so there were eight of us sharing ours. (Incidentally, the Naylor family left when I was quite small; Mrs N ran off with the man next door.)

There were five houses in the yard or court, as they were called, and with two more like ours facing Cemetery Road, it meant eight houses sharing four WCs. Slop pails were a regular sight as everybody had to go "up the passage" to empty the said utensil from time to time. These houses, consisting of three rooms, were known as "house, chamber and garret". No kitchens unless you were lucky; mostly the sink was in the living room and everything happened there: washing, baking, eating, bathing in a zinc bath in front of the fire.

★ ★ ★

In her early days at school, Lilian Mary managed to persuade people that she much preferred to be called Mary, so Mary she became. She remembered learning letters by chalking them on small blackboards and the bewilderment of playtime, bread and milk being passed through the railings, like "feeding the animals in the zoo". She had expensive tastes, apparently, and used her spending money to buy Rowntree's fruit gums. Her 1d only ran to three of the sweets. She wore clothes made by Auntie Annie that were always too big so she could 'grow into them' and black wool stockings knitted by her grandmother. She resented these 'funny' old-fashioned clothes, but some children came to school practically in rags and shoeless.

29

However: "nobody looked down on these kids and we were asked to bring shoes and clothes in for these unfortunates."

Later, she would recall the antics of boys with peashooters at Whit Monday processions, celebrations in the park and going to Sunday School at Cemetery Road Baptist Church. One of the highlights was when Uncle Bill acquired his first car, a Morris Oxford Coupe registration number PF 3364 needed for his job as a commercial traveller – a sales rep.

★ ★ ★

In the early months of 1939 there was much activity among the nations of Europe – treaties being signed which meant very little, the Spanish war ended, Italy seized Albania. Conscription was introduced into Britain in April and in the same month Hitler denounced the Anglo-German Naval Agreement and the Polish Non-Aggression Treaty. Mr Chamberlain reaffirmed the British pledge to Poland and altogether the outlook was ominous.

We all began to make preparations for what seemed now to be almost inevitable. I joined a First Aid post at Cemetery Road Vestry Hall, went to lectures on First Aid and gained a certificate from St John's Ambulance.

However, we (Dad and Mum, Uncle Bill and I) had planned to go away on the 7th of August. Three days before that, Joe (boyfriend) took me to the Speedway, a new experience for me. I was sad that I wouldn't see Joe for three weeks – he was going to camp and we were to go on holiday.

On the last Sunday of August, we'd been back a week and Joe came back from camp. He brought me a lovely compact and I gave him a snap of me taken on Dartmoor, which he said he had with him all through the war – and through his marriage!

It's very difficult to describe my feelings during the few days before the war started. I still clung to the hope that somehow peace would prevail, Mr Chamberlain would manage to pull something out of the hat and Hitler would withdraw from Poland, but it was a vain hope. On Friday 1ˢᵗ of September, there was general mobilisation. Joe had promised to meet me, but I thought because of being called up he wouldn't make it and I felt wretched and went to bed. Fortunately, Mother went outside into the road and saw him waiting there and brought him in. I came downstairs in my blue linen dress, and we all had supper together. I was very happy and knew then that I really cared for him.

On the Saturday I went to play tennis, but everyone was depressed, on edge and I came home early. At church on Sunday, Mr Chamberlain's message was relayed during the service, which ended early… "consequently we are at war with Germany."

Next day it was work as usual, but we were all at sixes and sevens and concerned about the blackout. The Athenia[6] was sunk.

Tuesday was about the worst day of my life! At night after I went to bed, Dad brought me up a letter from Joe (he had asked his sister to deliver it for him). My first love letter!

During the night there was an air raid alarm, and the wardens came round with rattles, which signified that poison gas bombs had

---

6   SS Athenia was a transatlantic passenger liner built in Glasgow in 1923. She worked between the UK and Canada. She was the first UK ship to be sunk, hit by a torpedo from a German submarine with the loss of 128 civilian passengers and crew. Until January 1946 German authorities denied that one of their vessels was responsible.

been dropped. I felt so ill I was physically sick and thought the end of the world had come. The whole thing turned out to be a false alarm.

During the next few weeks, Joe and I saw each other quite often but presently he had to join his regiment, the Royal Artillery, and life carried on as usual, the war seeming unreal and far away. I felt we meant a great deal to each other but before long he wrote to me saying he didn't think we should become committed because of the uncertainties of war. I felt rejected and hated him for a while, but didn't become unduly depressed – I was too busy at home and work, in life at Brunswick (Methodist Church), working at my First Aid, etc.

We were kept busy at BTH[7]. Most of the men had been called up (mind you, we managed quite well without them!). We carried on our social gatherings and became used to the blackout, still going to the cinema and so on. When the air raids in Britain started in earnest, we became more cautious and prepared. Coventry was the heaviest early raid in November 1940 followed by Bristol, Merseyside and Southampton. When would it be our turn? We were beginning to dread those moonlit nights.

We were getting used to the drone of the German bombers after the sirens had gone most evenings and for some time they had been targeting Liverpool and Manchester, so we were not expecting anything dramatic when the wail of the sirens went on the 12th of December. It was a Thursday evening and our little fellowship group from Brunswick were going to Dronfield Woodhouse with our minister Leslie Robinson (Robbo) to lead a short midweek service in which we were all to take

7   British Thomson-Houston, an electrical engineering and heavy
      industrial company where Mum worked as a typist.

part. It was a clear, frosty night with a 'bombers' moon', but even when we came out of the little village chapel, we were not aware that such devastation was taking place so near. I was the only one who said I could smell burning as soon as we started back, and then we all realised what was happening. As we came down Meadowhead we could see huge fires over the town. Robbo was clearly shaken but we all pressed on, wondering why we were the only people on the road, not a soul about, no cars, most eerie. As we were driving down Woodseats Road, we could actually hear bombs whistling down around us. We turned round and tumbled out of the car at the house of one of our church members. We spent the rest of the night in his cellar. It was a huge cellar and well fitted out as an air raid shelter. It was an eye opener for us as there was a vast store of food and everything one could want if an emergency lasted for weeks. We were all well stocked up at home but never on such a grand scale. Dr Kay and his wife were most kind and kept us fed and watered so we all kept our spirits up as best we could throughout the thunderous din of the bombing.

At last, the 'All Clear' went and we were able to continue our journey home. It took us ages to get down to the town – it was chaotic everywhere – the roads, pavements, everywhere was strewn with debris. It was difficult to find a clear space to drive – Robbo was obviously terrified as we all were and apprehensive as to what we might find when we eventually arrived home. The smell of burning was horrific and seemed to envelop everyone for months to come. Somehow, we negotiated our way through an appalling tangle of hosepipes, past fire engines, overturned trams and blazing cars. Once Robbo had dropped us near his home, the rest of us picked our way gingerly homewards along the cold, debris-strewn streets, past blazing houses and shops.

I was quite calm at this stage and quite expected to see my home destroyed and Mother and Father too. I made up my mind I would go to the Clarks' (Auntie Ada and Uncle Ernest) where I was sure they would take me in. However, miracles do happen, and they were all safe and sound at 48 Cemetery Road, though there was a large coping stone through the roof, which had landed on a bed in the attic. Uncle Bill was okay too. He had sheltered on Ecclesall Road on his way home from his weekly card-playing session. The next-door neighbours had come into our house with their two small children and all the family gathered on the cellar head. It was a wonderful feeling that we were all still alive. The bombs had been very near and the Moor (a main shopping street just around the corner) was completely gutted. Our windows were all blown in and there was no way we could think of sleeping there that night.

In the end, many city people who had friends in the suburbs trekked out to find temporary shelter on the west of the city where there had been relatively little damage. We went to stay with Miss Smith in Ringinglow Road – I don't think we were very welcome, but she put up with us for a couple of nights – afterwards, I stayed with Rene – a friend from work who lived on Springfield Avenue – and eventually Grandma Walker went to stay with Auntie Edith and family, and we had B&B at Mrs Barker's in Springfield Road. This was all very traumatic for us – the air raids were still spasmodic and the first weekend we were in Springfield Road a bomb demolished a house just down the road.

Time passed and, after about three months, we began looking for a house – there was no way we wanted to go back to No 48. We could have bought lovely houses for as little as £500, but Dad, ever cautious, thought it too risky and eventually Uncle Bill's boss, Mr Chandler, decided to move out of Sheffield and we rented their house –

54 Westwood Road. I never wanted to come here but who was I to be considered – and I'm still here… (in 2002).

Sheffield continued to pull itself together after the bombing when over 500 people were killed. The repairs and demolition carried on, shops relocated, some – at least three – took over cinemas. Walsh's, which was completely burnt out, carried on trading at the Mount at Broomhill.

Meanwhile, I was still at BTH in Campo Lane and life went on as usual.

1942 – the tide of war was turning in our favour with thousands of bombing raids on Germany and Rommel in retreat in the desert. My best friend Dorothy and I had been in 'reserved occupations' so far but we were both anxious to join up in the WAAF. However, it seemed to be a long, drawn-out process until after we went on holiday to Oxford again. Soon after this, Dorothy was called up and became a Wireless Operator in the WAAF. Late in 1943, I went for my medical to Bramall Lane Cricket Club as it was then and passed A1 for the WRNS – the Women's Royal Naval Service.

The adventure of joining the Wrens was a watershed in my life and the 15th of February 1944 was the great day when Mary Walker became a probationary Wren. We had a list of things we needed to take with us and one of them was a shoulder bag. It so happened that Uncle Bill was chatting to Mr Brothwell, our saddler friend who had a shop at Bridgehouses, and Mr B said he would make me a leather shoulder bag and mentioned in passing that he was making one for another girl who was joining the Wrens on the same day. This turned out to be Josie Johnson; we met and arranged to go together, meeting at Victoria Station, and we have remained friends ever since. We shared a cabin at

Lowton St Mary's near Warrington for the next six months whilst we trained to be wireless telegraphists (WTs).

For the first two weeks, our probationary period, we wore our civilian clothes and were free to leave at the end of the two weeks if we didn't feel we fitted in. I didn't know of anyone who left, however, and at the end of the fortnight we all felt part of the Navy and were issued with our kit. Then came the task of lengthening or shortening skirts, jackets and raincoats until we had achieved that perfect fit. We learned how to wear our hats at the correct angle, to tie our shoelaces correctly, to salute, and a thousand and one things about life in the Royal Navy, including all the naval expressions like splicing the mainbrace, swinging the lamp Sam, wearing your Tiddly suit[8] and many more.

There were coders, WT Wrens and Visual Signallers (VS) training with us at HMS Cabbala and also men coders. Jo and I shared a cabin with a VS Wren who had changed categories and been a long time in the Wrens. Her name was Sylvia and came from "the South". She was a bit of a pain, though harmless; she thought she knew it all. However, we felt some sympathy for her as she had the most awful chilblains down the front of both legs in spite of being able, as a VS Wren, to wear bell-bottoms.

Of course, we had to go through the routine of vaccination and poor Jo had the most awful arm. She had vaccine fever and was really very ill in sickbay and has the bad scarring to this day.

We were in classes of about twenty to twenty-five and we were in the Windsor class. All the WT classes had names of destroyers – Warwick, Wessex and Worcester and the coders had C names like Calliope, Ceres, whilst the VS ones were Venus, Ventura, etc. Our

---

8   Respectively: handing out the ration of rum, telling an old sailor's yarn, wearing your best uniform.

PO Wren who taught us the Morse Code was Kay Spikings, a nice lass who came from Scunthorpe. We were a motley crew who hailed from as far afield as Cornwall, Dumfries, Dundee and Kent. Some girls had only just left boarding school at seventeen, whilst I was the oldest in the class at nearly twenty-four.

★ ★ ★

Our first long leave was due in the first week of June and we knew something was afoot when it was rumoured that all leave was cancelled. However, we were able to go home but not able to use the train. Somehow, everyone managed to hitch a lift and Jo, Pat and I were picked up by an RAF lorry and dropped in Manchester. From there we took a bus to Hyde and from there to Glossop. On the outskirts of Glossop, we three intrepid Wrens started walking towards Sheffield. We'd only gone a few yards when a car pulled up and offered us a lift to Sheffield. The man was a representative at Met-Vicks and knew quite a lot of people I knew. It was a great run and we saw the extended Ladybower reservoir with the bridge newly opened, which we had never seen before.

The day after we arrived home was D Day with all the excitement and tremendous movement that it involved. We really felt then that we were winning the war at last, and all wondered how much longer it would go on for. By the end of our week's leave, we were allowed to use the train again and, when we returned to HMS Cabbala, we began to get ready for our exams. We had a lot of electrical theory to learn, and I hadn't really a clue what it was all about, physics never being my strong point, but I managed it somehow, learning a lot of it by heart, which paid off in the end.

I think most of our class passed our final exam (the odd ones that didn't were transferred to another course) and we had the inevitable party, which was held at Newton le Willows a few miles away. The NZ air force contingent was stationed nearby and were our guests, and a good time was had by all.

We had some choice as to where we wanted to go but, obviously, we had to take potluck. Betty Burnett and I were very friendly by this time and, as there were postings to the headquarters of the Home Fleet at Scapa Flow, I joined with her and Flo and Pat and three others and opted for the far north.

That first journey to Thurso was an adventure in itself – more than 800 miles from Manchester. Sometimes we had to change trains at Edinburgh, or Perth, or both. On the journey to Thurso through the night, there was a wonderful canteen on the train run by the Salvation Army. It was always crowded, and adventurous people sometimes slept on the luggage rack. I was never so hard up for a seat as all that. As the dawn broke and we stretched our legs and staggered down the corridor, we gazed out at a desolate landscape, grey and flat and treeless, and we felt we might be in Siberia for all we knew. The Wrennery at Thurso just by the station welcomed us with a delicious breakfast. This was a wonderful thing in wartime for they still gave you bacon and eggs and lovely bread and jam, something unheard of in England but somehow always available in Scotland where high tea was still the norm.

Much refreshed, the Wrens were taken by bus to Scrabster Harbour to board the ferry to Lyness (the naval base on Hoy). All the ferries and fishing boats had been commandeered by the government in wartime.

It was a cold, dull August morning as we approached the islands and we wondered what bleak future was in store for us, but as we came

Wren Mary Walker

in sight of Lyness, the sun streamed down, welcoming us to Orkney with its warmth.

A minibus met us to take us up to our quarters, HMS Haybrake, normally about ten minutes on foot. Our cabins were rather like old hospital wards. Thank goodness not double bunks – watchkeepers were spared that. There were sixteen beds in our cabin and all seven of us (from HMS Cabbala) were together. We soon found our way around our new home and the next day we went on duty at Wee Fea, the communications centre of the Home Fleet. It was a gaunt, forbidding building built deep in the hillside. We were taken up the hill to work each day by buggy (minibus), which usually picked up the men first as their quarters were quite a distance from ours. Betty Burnett and I were on the same watch, and we worked thus:

- Afternoon and last dog noon–4pm and 6–8pm.
- Forenoon and first 8am–noon and 8pm–2am.
- First dog and morning 4–6pm and 2am–8am.
- Then a day off until next day at noon.

5

Settling In

Wren Tel L.M.Walker 94167
WRNS Quarters
HMS Haybrake
RN Base
Lyness
Orkney
14th September

My dear Mum and all,

It was lovely to get your letters and I hope you are not having too many worries, except waiting for the letter from the hospital, Dad. Next time you send a parcel, Mum, will you put in my winter pyjamas, the pink ones and the blue ones, because I think I shall be wanting them before long now.

We had the afternoon off yesterday and went ship visiting. This was a very interesting new experience. We started out at about 2.30pm and went out in a drifter[9] to the ship. Certain ratings and officers were detailed off to take us round and we saw a great many interesting things; it was great fun climbing up and down ladders, I wish you could have seen us.

---

9   A drifter is a former fishing boat that has been requisitioned for use by the forces.

We had tea in their mess and the sailors flocked around and cut bread and butter and made the tea. We saw everything we could. I always imagined ships to be great big dark grey things, but some of them – camouflaged, of course – are the most glorious colours, pale green, bright blue and pale bluey green and beautiful, really. We went inside the great gun turrets and saw all the vast mechanism which goes into the operating of these deadly weapons – it was wonderful.

People in civvy street would give their last penny to see ships like we have been able to see for nothing. It's a marvellous experience and I wouldn't have missed it for anything. Don't worry about me going out in little boats – they are not little at all – and all have cabins down below quite like the type we were on at Brighton.

Today we have been out to the Flow again, to quite a different type, but a tremendous ship. We saw the Admiral's cabins, it was great fun.

Tomorrow it is our stand-off and Betty Burnett and I are going to Kirkwall, the capital of the islands. It takes a couple of hours. We two are on the same watch so we shall be able to go out when we are off duty.

Have had a letter from Dorothy Rob. She is still at the holding depot and is pulling as many strings as possible to try and get drafted here. I hope she manages it. Josie has apparently been sent to Milford Haven with Mary H who we all disliked very much, so I'm doubly thankful I came up here, I'm sure I did the right thing, for once. Jo would be furious because she did not want to go to South Wales, she wanted to stay at Plymouth.

Am going to bed now. Will write more tomorrow. Goodnight lovies.

It is now Monday night and I have just come back from Kirkwall and received your letter, Dad. Am very happy to know that when you receive this letter the horrible suspense will be over and you will have the worst of the nasty business over. What a wonderful relief that will be for all of you. I know you will worry now but don't, Mum, dear. I'll be thinking about you all the time, especially tonight when I don't suppose you'll have much sleep – and don't forget when it's over you must have a holiday, Mum and Uncle Bill – try to get the shop window done while Dad is away, even if you have to pay yourself for it.

Our trip to Kirkwall was really lovely. It was a perfect day with the sun shining and was really mild. It took about one and a half hours, it's a grand trip. You are never in the open sea here, it is practically enclosed by islands. You pass all the ships, big and little, at anchor, and the hills covered with heather and the gentle corn-covered slopes sweeping down to the sea form a very lovely background – it's just like being on holiday. Kirkwall is a quaint little town, and it was very pleasant to see houses and shops again. Everything was lovely and clean, and the houses are of a clean grey stone and reminded me rather of Cornwall. The streets are very narrow, and the shops are very quaint and old-fashioned. What I did notice was a number of shops with white enamelled dishes and bowls and quite a lot of things of that nature. We went round the cathedral, which seems to be built of some sort of red sandstone and is very old.

We had a good dinner and an even better tea with sausage, egg and chips and bread and butter – about half a pound of it – and scones and pancakes, as much as you could eat for 1/9d. There was also ice cream, but we hadn't time for any.

All these trips by the way are free, we can hop about as we like to these various places. Tonight we feel really tired. All this sea air makes me hungry and I am eating like a horse. Last night, for instance, when we came back from the ship, we went into supper after having tea on *the ship – and there was crab pie, delicious, and lots of 'gash' (naval term for leftovers) including cold beef, potatoes and beetroot and we just helped ourselves. What a treat. You can just read this to Dad on Saturday, I'm sure he will appreciate it.*

Look out for the announcement of Dorothy's engagement in the papers. I wish she were here, she wouldn't be in such a hurry to get engaged then!!!! Too much choice of men for that…

Well, my old ducks, I must go and have a bath now so,
   Lots of love,
   Mary

I'm amused by Mum's dispatching of St Magnus cathedral with one sentence. The most wonderful, atmospheric, evocative place, built in 1137, and all she can say is it seems to be built of some sort of red sandstone and is old! Whereas when it comes to food, she'll wax lyrical for pages. Shows what was preoccupying her mind in that time of war – especially after the shortages in Sheffield.

And the emphasis on the clean stone of the Kirkwall houses. The clean air can still be noticed here; people who travel south all talk of the pall of pollution they notice hanging in the air once they get as far south as Manchester. In those days, though, it would have been really striking because Sheffield Cathedral, along with the other buildings in the city centre, was completely black, covered with the smoky sooty outpourings of the industrial city. For me, as a child in the fifties and sixties, that was simply how they were; I thought black was the colour of the brick and stone. When the sandblasting clean-up started following the Clean Air Act in the seventies and the bright, scrubbed stone emerged, it was an utter revelation.

Wren Tel L.M.Walker 94167
WRNS Quarters
HMS Haybrake
RN Base
Lyness
Orkney
24/9/44

My dear Dad,

I know you will appreciate a few lines, my old duck, and I hope you'll be able to read my atrocious writing, it's bad enough reading it with two good eyes, but I've no doubt someone will read it to you if you can't.

Well, you know how glad I am that the job's done and, according to Mum's letters, it's not nearly as bad as you expected, and I hear everyone is very kind and helpful. I have your letters, which you wrote home before the (ahem!!) "happy event", and I was glad to hear you were feeling much better than when I left home. I expect the worst part of the business is lying in bed all day but I've no doubt that by this time you will be able to get about a little each day.

I have just met a sailor from Sheffield on the same watch as me – he lives at Southey Green and used to be on the old Handsworth car[10] route.

I have heard from Dorothy Farrow this week. I had not heard for so long I had begun to think she had eloped with Tim, but she has had

---

10 'Car' means tramcar here.

mumps and has not been allowed to write any letters for two weeks.

These last two weeks I have had very little mail and complained about it in my last two letters home, so I think Mum must have told people as I have had a bumper crop of letters during the weekend.

It's Sunday afternoon now and I'm writing this during a quiet spell on watch. I hope you'll forgive me if I tell you what you've already heard from the family letters. I wrote a long letter this morning, so no doubt you'll have another repetition on Saturday when Mum comes over.

It is Monday afternoon now and we have just been to the cinema. Unfortunately, I couldn't get this finished yesterday. We became quite busy, so I had to leave my writing. The film we've just seen was awfully funny, I'm looking forward to seeing the next one at the end of the week "A Canterbury Tale".

Betty has just had a parcel of sweets and homemade toffees, they are grand and a change from the ordinary plain chocolate. (They are just playing a selection from Lilac Time – I wonder if you are listening, my old duck?)

Did I tell you we had Yehudi Menuhin up here? It was really great. I see there is a music lovers' circle, and we are hoping to go to one of the concerts next week.

I'm hoping you are not going to be long going back to the 'old firm' or I can see me wearing out my tiddly shoes. This place isn't ideal for leather soles. I've already worn my gumboots and oilskins but usually it's been a case of locking the stable door when the horse has gone. (I can't get on with this letter, Dad, there's a girl who will insist on sitting on the bed at the side of me and she is a bit of a 'drip'.)

She's gone now, so I'll continue. I was just telling you about the climate. Today, for instance, it was raining like h--- and I had on my best hat when a sudden gust of wind blew it off into a ditch, flat in the mud. Of course I went after it and sank up to my ankles in mud, this sort of thing is quite frequent. Even when it's a lovely sunny day, the peaty soil is always very wet. I think it's the peat that makes the water so funny. It is dark brown in colour and when you are having a bath it looks as though you are floating about in a bath of "old and mild".

That reminds me, while I'm writing to you, I may as well get you to ask Uncle Bill if he is able to supply me with a bath plug – none of the baths or basins here have them. If he can get one, I'll let him know the size.

We have met some very nice people who live in a tiny, thatched cottage on the island. They are not islanders, but Scottish folk, and Betty and I were there last Saturday to supper. It is a quaint little house, just the sort we have seen in pictures, typically Orcadian with grass growing on the roof and no upstairs, just a bed let into the wall off the dining room. Quaint old fireplace and oil lamps. We had to hurry back, unfortunately, as we are not allowed in that part of the island after blackout unless in an organised party. We are confined to quite a small boundary after blackout time, about a three-quarter-mile radius of the quarters – it's perhaps as well, really, because there's nothing to do except within three quarters of a mile anyway.

This last two weeks seems to have been mostly sleeping, working and eating. It has taken us quite a time to get used to the irregular hours, getting up at 1am and going to bed at 8am, but we are quite accustomed to it now and we are going to try and make up for our lack of entertainment by going to two dances and two films this week. We haven't done any ship visiting for over a fortnight but are hoping to go on Sunday if there is a decent ship in.

Some of our girls going on watch at 2am the other night saw the Northern Lights, but we were fast asleep. Apparently, they are to be seen quite often here being so far north. However, we have seen some really lovely skies since we have been here; there seems to be such a vast expanse of glorious colour and we get high winds, which make them still more lovely.

Betty and I went for a lovely walk last week onto the moors. We managed to find a skeleton of a sheep almost intact. We walked back on the beach and did a bit of beach combing. There are some funny things to be found washed up – letters (very interesting), hats, boots, hot water bottles, and a whole collection of stuff thrown overboard by ships. As we were coming back, I naturally skipped across the 'burn' by the stepping stones but, of course, stepped on a wobbly one and my old hat sailed into the water and I went into the water with the water over my ankles. Fortunately, it's only a shallow stream, so I soon retrieved my hat.

Actually, the water was only about three inches deep and there was an RN officer fishing. Complete with rod and gumboots. I can't think what he expected to catch except minnows.

Well, Dad, I hope you are managing to read this – if you can, you are a better man than I am Gunga Din.

Went to the dentists on Friday – every time I go there, he injects, even though it's only for filling. I could scarcely open my mouth for two days. What did you say? Good job? I can assure you, it didn't stop me eating

– or talking. I'm going to have my teeth scaled and polished tomorrow on my day off.

Well, old duck, I'll have to go to work again, so I'll have to leave. I do hope you're okay, love. I'm sure you'll be thankful when you're home again. I've been saying you must have a holiday.

 Heaps of love,
 Mary Xxxx Xxxx[11]

The 'happy event' or, as she said in the earlier letter, the 'nasty business' that befell my grandfather, I suppose, was cataract surgery, which in those pre-implant days would have left him without a lens in his eye at all, so he had to wear thick glasses. As a cobbler, he needed to be able to see what he was doing. At that time, he must have been well past retirement age, but seemingly intended to carry on working for the old firm, which he'd run with his father. What does she mean *even if you have to pay yourself for it?* Does she mean them paying someone else to do it, or them paying themselves to do it? Was it the window that was blown out during the blitz in Sheffield and needed repairing? Surely that would already have been mended. Or did she mean cleaning up and rearranging things? And why didn't I ask all these things while she was alive?

Imagine being confined to bed after a cataract operation! Now it's a day job, in and out in less than two hours, as I well know, having inherited the condition at a relatively young age. When my mother had her cataracts done in the early 1970s,

---

11   The censor must have eased up by this point, since from now on Mary often adds kisses!

she also stayed in hospital and had no lens implant. She struggled with huge heavy glasses that made her nose sore, or a giant contact lens that rubbed on the scar tissue of the cornea. She described seeing astonishing colours during the operation, done under local anaesthetic, as different layers of the eye were opened up. (I'd been looking forward to that part when my turn came, but was rather underwhelmed by the experience.) Once, on her way to work at a local primary school, the contact lens popped out. I followed in her footsteps an hour later and amazingly found it – it was that big – in the middle of the road, having been squashed by a car.

How lucky I am, forty years later, to have two new lens implants and almost perfect eyesight, except for needing reading glasses, but I can live with that.

6

July

By July, the cows (kye) are knee-deep in buttercups and the irises are out. The verges and ditches are stiff with budding meadowsweet, plantain (known in Orkney as "soldiers") with their lacy midriffs, and curly doddies. These last are red clover. "I don't know what doddies are," said Margaret Miller, "and I don't know what is curly about these ones, but…"

The curlews have changed their behaviour and are in chick-minding mode. What is a curlew chick called: a curling? The parents spend their time perched on fence posts or walls, surveying the scene and keeping an eye out for the youngsters, two of whom wander around my garden without a care in the world. The farmer cut the meadow in front of the house, and I was astonished that evening to look out and see the curlews had taken over. I counted at least 100 before giving up. They must have thought the fridge door had been left open and they were raiding the goodies. The curlews had first dibs, top of the probing order; by next morning most of them had gone and a fleet of oystercatchers had moved in. Skylarks burst up into the sky.

Over the marshy, undrained fields at the back, a flock of lapwings rises, pulsating and throbbing, beating as if one body; if it were music, it would be vibrato. Starlings continue the theme and arrange themselves along the wires in musical notation, although the tune they make would be somewhat monotonous; smaller birds make a more interesting cluster of notes, but shorter.

Life in Orkney is organised by the weekly paper *The Orcadian*, a free monthly magazine *The Orkney Advertiser*, and Facebook. There are numerous Facebook groups, including Orkney Sky, Rock on Orkney, Orkney Wildflowers, Orkney Birds, Orkney Wildlife, Orkney Snorkelling, Orkney Photography and no doubt others that I haven't discovered yet.

Sorry to say, having spurned Facebook for some time in activity terms, anyway – I've now become a bit of a fan. One of the groups I'm in is the Orkney Polar Bear Group, for those who like sea swimming. They have a regular Saturday swim, as well as impromptu dips whenever anyone feels like mentioning them. Having joined the group, I delayed meeting them for a swim, being deterred by the drizzle, rain or gales that were accompaniments to every Saturday morning. I did swim, though, on my own, when the weather was good.

One of my swim spots was the Bay of Skaill – conveniently my nearest beach. I'd been warned about 'a bit of an undertow' there, so cautiously got in the water at one end, sheltered from the wind, with flat sand and no waves; cold, of course – very – but exhilarating, thrilling and invigorating.

Later that week, something else to frighten me off: in the newspaper was a report of a woman being trapped in quicksand at that very same beach. The coastguard was called out:

> "… to the aid of a woman at the beach at around 10.20pm. Arriving on the scene, the rescue team found that the woman, with the help of a man, had managed to free herself from the sand.
>
> The public are being warned of a potential sinkhole at the Bay of Skaill, Sandwick, after the incident."

According to Orkney Islands Council the area has been cordoned off while the hole is being looked into.

Another opportunity for voluntary work that is occupying me is at Steptoze Yard, a recycling/reuse scheme supported by a charity called Zerowaste Scotland, who promote reduction of household waste by encouraging and educating people to reuse and recycle. In effect, Steptoze Yard is the last stop before the tip, a cross between a charity shop and the dump. Housed in a shipping container, a portacabin and a caravan is a motley collection of people's rubbish: old diving equipment, children's books, PlayStation 2 games, rusty nails, spare tyres, old toilets, sinks and window frames, a rather nice cot circa 1950 (probably with lead paint), office chairs, faded pictures in chipped frames, many plant pots, a Babyliss male grooming kit, a baby alarm, two long thin plastic chickens wearing red plastic bras and pants (! Some kind of esoteric cooking aid?), sundry plastic plumbing bits and five huge bales of plastic milk bottle tops. The latter had been collected by well-meaning folk for charitable reasons over the years. I have a vague memory of a scheme to provide wheelchairs for children if one could raise the weight of the child in plastic milk bottle tops. The scheme has long since fizzled out, but habits die hard and people can't seem to stop collecting the things. How to get rid of them? One of the volunteers hits on the idea of smuggling them in sealed bags to the tip, where they will be shipped to Shetland and incinerated along with the other unsalvageable rubbish from Orkney.

Now, I'm not known as the most clutter-free person; as one friend remarked on entering a house I'd recently moved into, "It's not taken you long to Tyzackise it." But, post-Africa and house moving, even I would draw the line at hanging on to many of the items to be found at Steptoze Yard; after all, the council 'recycling centre' is just around the corner. "You'd be surprised what folk'll buy," said the boss, Mr Steptoe, when I venture to mutter as much to him. "I'm constantly amazed." One day, a woman came in looking for a plastic barrel so that she could make a temporary septic tank. She was moving to a derelict house in the wilds of Westray to rebuild it – or activities to that effect – and went away fairly contented with part of a compost cone for the contents of her 'toilet' (will I be able to dig a deep enough hole, she mused) and a watering can that she planned to use as a shower, in a barn with no roof. Personally, in the absence of a proper shower, I always preferred a big bucket, a mug and a lot of splashing.

One positively successful recycling project is ScrapStore. This involves supplying local primary schools with certain carefully selected items of junk and putting them in a

'Playpod' for the children to take out and use at playtime. The most popular items are old vacuum cleaners, huge plastic barrels like water butts, suitcases, laptops, computer keyboards, netting, dressing-up clothes and long cardboard roll inners that used to have carpet wrapped round them. Basically, anything that could possibly be played with and adapted by an imaginative primary school child. I therefore spend one day each week washing out old vacuum cleaners and their hoses, cutting off cables to make them safe for the kids to use. And scrubbing old gutters. What an exciting life I have!! The barrels used to contain picric acid used by farmers for something or other, so have to be neutralised and washed out well before consigning them to the PlayPod. After years of health and safety regulations, the teachers and assistants have to readjust their ideas of risk, and the children love it. One day, we did a ScrapStore drop at Papdale Primary School in Kirkwall, the biggest of the Orkney primary schools. The playground was impressive, with a replica Ring of Brodgar, a circle of standing stones for the children to climb on, amongst other things. We pulled up outside the PlayPod and a few kids (in the playground even in the school holiday) excitedly gathered round to watch us unloading. "Look," whispered one, "a pushchair!" Amazing, isn't it? Kids in Tanzania will make toys out of whatever old rubbish they can find – wheels, bits of wood, tyres, and so will kids in Orkney. It's just there's more rubbish here. Or rather, more expensive rubbish.

As we sat in the sun on the caravan step eating our lunch, Steptoe nodded across towards the garage opposite. "See over there, to the right of O's? There's a grit box. I'm sure there's something dodgy going on." He explained that there's a regular 'dead letter box' drop; a bus comes along, the driver unloads a few boxes into the grit box and, sometime later, various shady looking people turn up in 4x4s, take out a parcel and beat a rapid retreat. What could it be – drugs? Money?

Eventually, bumping into Linnet the garage owner's wife, encouraged by me, he asks her what's going on. Disappointingly, it's car parts ordered by other garages from the car parts factories. What a sensible way to go about delivering them.

Apart from recycling, Mr Steptoe's other interest is in flying things – mainly birds and damsels; the feathered variety of the former and the ones related to dragonflies of the latter. I'd be there round the back, hosing down a lost traffic cone with the steam cleaner – my newly discovered favourite power tool – and there'd come a cry from the caravan door: "Jings! Look at that! An Arctic skua being mobbed by a flock of starlings!" I've looked up in time to miss all sorts, from house martins to peregrines, which he's amazingly quick to spot, possibly as a result of his previous career in army surveillance methods.

The great skuas, or bonxies as they are called here, are particularly nasty. I know nature is red in tooth and claw and everything has to live, but really! Walking with a friend on the tidal island of Brough of Birsay, there's a great commotion, a screeching and squawking on the cliffs below. A bonxie flies out to sea with something white and flappy dangling. It takes the white flappy dangly thing, a kittiwake or a fulmar, I can't tell which, down onto the gentle waves, where it's joined by a friend, a fellow bonxie. Between them, they hold the other bird under the surface and proceed to pluck it. Pluck it!! Somehow, this nicety is more horrible than the actual killing and eating. It suggests a rather delicate, finicky, *human* side to the whole business. The pair of predators jab at the prey, pulling out the feathers and tossing them over their shoulders, a white downy flutter drifting behind them on the breeze. We can only see white, with the ripples washing over it, and suddenly they're through the skin and a flush of red blooms over the white body. Surely the bird must have drowned by now. We watch, spellbound by the horror, and eventually move on, shocked by what looks like brutality. It's a tough life.

A family of pied wagtails has made themselves at home around the house. The outside of the house, I hasten to add. Three of the young – pale and a bit fluffy still – pester their parents for food, although they are already tail-wagging and appear to be quite capable of feeding themselves. In the sunny mornings, they sit on the front wall, bobbing and preening. The parents have taken to masquerading as hummingbirds in their fly-catching behaviour, performing impressive displays of acrobatic manoeuvering and hovering above my thistles. Occasionally I've heard a soft thud against the window as a confused bird of some sort bats against it. There are swallows, meadow pipits and linnets, breasts blushing fit to burst, but I don't know who it is banging on the window.

The garden is fast becoming a crèche. Young swallows

arrange themselves along my clothesline, mouths gaping as a parent swoops in. A pipit parent attempts to stuff something daddy-long-leggy into an infant's mouth. Baby wrens churr and chirrup, scuttling in the willows.

At last, whilst wagtail watching, I spotted an Orkney vole. There are lots of well-used tunnels in the garden but this one popped out of a hole in the stone wall, scuttled along a bit and popped back in: a little dark grey job with no apparent head or tail. Another time, as a friend and I watched from the kitchen window, a vole in a hurry made a dash for its hole from behind the oil tank. On the way, though, it passed a dandelion that was obviously too good to miss; it backtracked, bit off the dandelion flower and carried it swiftly back to the safety of home.

Stromness Shopping Week, towards the end of July, came and went without making much noticeable impression apart from the bunting: where else would you find ladies' knickers strung across the main street? A banner announced: "67 years of bunting and now it's just pants". One tongue-in-cheek shop window bore a notice: Stromness Summerwear Sale, beside a display of wet weather gear, gloves and woolly hats. There was a Shopping Week Queen who, with her attendants, valiantly braved less than clement weather in her queen's gown to open a few events and visit old folks' homes. A children's fancy dress three-legged race drew a bit of a crowd. But the main event was a Viking torch-lit procession through the town to the tautological Point of Ness, where a Viking longship was dramatically hurled blazing down the slip in the gathering dusk, before everyone repaired to the Royal Hotel, The Ferry Inn, or home.

Towards the end of the month, a hen pheasant and two chicks wandered past my window. It looked like their first walk, as they gave jittery, nervous glances around. I was delighted to see the kye in my field. It can't be used for grazing any earlier because of the ground nesting birds, but now it's safe for the cattle to trample all over to their hearts' content. The calves are getting skittish and teenagerish; they buck and butt, playfully locking heads and kicking up their heels, but still run back to Mum for a suckle. Not exactly teenagerish then, and they don't like it much if they suddenly find themselves on the wrong side of the fence from their mother and can't get back. There's also a big brown bull who seems very popular with the cows. They nuzzle his face and lick his neck, while he just stands there and tolerates it. I hadn't realised cattle were that romantic.

7

To Wee Fea

I hadn't expected so much emotion. It was meant to be purely a research trip, but turned into what felt like a pilgrimage.

Taking advantage of a sunny day near the end of August, thinking it might well be the best day of the fast-declining summer, I took the ferry from Houton on the north coast of Scapa Flow to Lyness on the Hoy coast. This was the naval base where Mum and more than 1500 fellow Wrens were based in WWII, as well as several thousand other troops. During the tourist season, there are guided walks around what remains of the base. It was a funny feeling, sitting quietly on the narrow open passenger deck, listening to the summer visitors wondering whether they have on enough clothes for a day on Hoy, and to their talk of orcas sighted passing the Ness campsite. I knew Mum would have been up on deck, not in the downstairs passenger lounge, so I stayed there too.

At the visitor centre, there's just enough time for a pot of tea before the tour, and I glance through the leaflet about the site.

Wee Fea, the hill behind the base, still has a large concrete fortress-like building dominating the scene. "*This was the main Naval Headquarters and Communications Centre and it was here that*

Wee Fea Communications Centre

many of the WRNS worked." Including my mum. Reading this, I'm astonished to feel my eyes pricking, the tears threatening. Surely I can't cry over my tea and scone?

Quickly finishing the tea, I join the dozen or so people waiting outside with the guide, Jude, and we're off. There are two young children, about eight and six years old. I feel sorry for them, they are surely going to be bored rigid. It's a lovely day. We walk past the old dance hall, the cinema that seated about 500 where Mum used to go. It's falling to pieces, the corrugated iron caving in and flapping in the gentle breeze, and probably can't last another winter. "No money to restore it," sighs Jude. Up past Haybrake, where the WRNS lived – that's the ablutions block, that's the old post office where

Mum would have given in her letters for posting and, away up on the hill, the imposing communications centre still stands, stark and forbidding on this bright day. Jude remembers when there were linen charts still on the walls, but people have taken them and scavenged all sorts of things. Now, she says, it's dank and dark; animals have been in there and it's unsafe.

We make our way round to the naval cemetery and eventually back to the museum. I head back up the hill, up Wee Fea to explore more. Mum would have been taken up the track in a truck or something, I imagine. It wouldn't be very good to have to walk up in all weathers and at all hours of the day and night for those watches. As I near the building, it rears up, more and more impressive. Just one window in the sheer concrete and sort of portholes all along, about two-thirds of the way up. On the top, a short look-out tower where the visual signallers used to go and wave flags. There's a 'Danger Keep Out' notice. I sit and eat a sandwich, and drink tea from my flask to gather courage to go in. Scapa Flow is spread out below me, blue and calm.

A flight of decaying outside steps leads up to a door. There are gaps in the stairs and I'm careful not to tread on the worst ones. Sheep droppings and mud on the floor at the entrance, and a view down a long corridor that I'm too nervous to explore in case I fall through.

So, I turn and go round to the bottom entrance, hoicking my leg over the concrete barrier that has been built, too late, to keep out the sheep. I too am looking for a memento. Someone's chalked an arrow on the wall, with the instruction 'In', so I follow. Inside, round the corner, it's pitch dark, and

I fumble in a pocket for my phone. With the flashlight on, it's better, but possibly even more spooky. I'm in the boiler room, where some joker has placed a sheep's skull on top of the old rusty furnace. There are dark oil stains on the floor and a partial skeleton. I don't stay long.

Souvenirs are in short supply, and sheep bones don't seem appropriate. Instead, I earmark a massive rust-eaten hinge and retreat to continue further up the hill.

At the top, fresh peat is drying in stacks, the blocks not yet stacked are separated by wooden markers, which reminded me of gravestones in the naval cemetery. Orkney is spread out to the north and east in a bright blue haze. The family from the guided tour appear in the distance and also have a mooch round the communications centre. When they've gone, I hike down, retrieve my prize and make my way back to the ferry, past the broken remnants of wartime piers along the roads echoing with ghosts of the thousands of men and women who laughed and cried and worked here in those war years.

Wren Tel L.M.Walker 94167
WRNS Quarters
HMS Haybrake
RN Base
Lyness
Orkney
9.10.44

My dear Mum and all,
I was thrilled tonight to receive your lovely long letter. We had been to Kirkwall, and we were very tired, and as soon as we had had

our suppers, we decided to have a hot bath. Just as I was going to the bathroom, Flo brought me three letters, it was a grand surprise. One was from Dorothy Robertson who is at Padstow, Cornwall, and the other from Beryl, all very lovely and newsy and which I read in the bath.

You seem to be quite busy these days, Mum, cleaning, etc. I hope you won't knock yourself out. Have you found anything in the way of hidden treasures?

I should think Dad would be coming home this week. I was glad to receive his letter. Don't let him go back to work too soon!!

Many thanks for all the titbits of news and all the information about the starch. Actually, I shall not be starching many because most of the WTs send theirs to the Cabbala laundry, so we have started sending ours along with theirs and, although it is about 2^d or 3^d a collar including postage, it is worth it because they are beautifully done. I only wish we could send our own laundry like that. It is a bit of a B… I have lost my pink pyjama top – the ones that Edith gave me – but I am wearing my winter ones now. Really, it's not terribly cold, but I didn't want to wear a thin pair and then a thick pair.

Betty and I have had a lovely time today. We went with Eleanor and Audrey and two girls on our watch to Kirkwall. We went on watch at 2am this morning and worked till 8am and then went to breakfast and intended to catch the 8.30am drifter. However, maddeningly enough, the blinking boat was just leaving the pier and we missed it by only a minute. There was an hour to wait before the next drifter, which was a provision boat not originally intended to carry passengers, but which always does. It was a most superb morning, the sunshine quite warm, streaming down on to the still water and the pink glow of the hills in the distance. Everything seemed very peaceful, the small tugs and little cargo boats chugged away merrily, their crews busy with the early morning deck swabbing. We had an hour to wait, so we walked up and down the pier watching the various little ships going to and fro and our particular boat being steadily loaded, mostly with beer barrels, which were placed all the way round the edge of the deck. Next came mineral waters and then empty laundry baskets and finally two tiny, frightened baby calves in sacks were deposited on the deck.

Whilst we were waiting, the most amazing 'thing' walked on to the pier – a Canadian Lieut RCN with a terrific black beard and what a moustache!! It was about six inches across but curled down instead of up. We had our eyes on him (and his companion, another Lieut) but our hopes of their company during the journey were thwarted when at the last minute our worst enemies – most horrible girls, the worst type of snobs – came up and turned on the charm. It was funny, though. Mum, you would laugh if you saw some of the girls' technique. However, I'll be able to tell you all about it when I see you – it's really too lengthy and involved, but you'd never believe what some of them are like. We have many a good laugh! I'll be able to tell you so much – I shall never stop talking when I am home. I have heard that all being well I'll be home <u>before</u> Xmas, so that's much better than I'd hoped for.

However, to get back to the subject. We had a really delightful trip, on the top of the beer barrels. It's lovely to see the ships, so many of them at anchor and the glorious hills in the background, some of them golden with harvest and then strips of green and yet again further along the hills covered with heather in the last stages of its beauty, sweeping down to the rocky cliffs.

Eventually, we arrived at Scapa Pier and proceeded to Kirkwall. I had wanted to buy a skirt – a tweed one to wear here (you can get *them on a pyjama chit) – but unfortunately I could not find one my size. But some of the tweeds and coats are so nice it seems a pity not to get one while we are here. What I think I will do, Mum, if you say it's okay, I will get another chit and buy a 'coat', a tweed one. They have some really nice ones and I <u>do</u> need one and they are not terribly expensive – I have already saved £5 since I have been here. What do you think of the idea?*

Will you have that navy and white checked skirt cleaned for me please, Mum? I want to wear it on leave – huh!! Anticipation!!!

We bought quite a lot of odds and ends and, of course, had a good lunch and tea, and it was such a nice sunny day.

We had to leave at 4.30 and, laden with all our bits of purchases, we clambered into the drifter. There were a good many sailors from the various ships coming back from Kirkwall and we had quite a lot of fun. They had a tremendous marrowbone for a very tiny dog – the dog wasn't nearly as big as the bone. It took ages to get back, depositing the various groups of sailors at their different ships. We were talking to quite a few fellows from Sheffield and district. The sun was just sinking as we approached the harbour and, a little before we arrived, we saw a school of porpoises – it was most interesting, the first time I have ever seen any. They were playing about for ages.

There are always lots of interesting things to be seen here. For instance, Dad would love to see the men from the big ships fishing from the deck and they always seem to catch quite a lot.

By the way, I haven't been anywhere to see any kippers, so I haven't been able to send you any. I would have loved to send Dad something from Kirkwall, but I couldn't think of anything he would want, can you?

Tuesday

I have just received the letter from Uncle Bill, many many many thanks for it, love, it was so nice, I am lucky to have such lovely letters. I am so sorry Dad is not coming home so soon and has to have another slight operation, but hope most fervently that it will be successful. He seems to be quite comfortable from all accounts, but I know you'll be very happy when he comes home.

Pat and Flo have been to Kirkwall and Flo has bought a lovely coat and Pat a skirt and jumper.

Unofficially, but I think <u>quite</u> likely, I'll be coming on leave in December (not Xmas) with Pat. Isn't that nice? We shall be able to travel together.

We were over a ship on Sunday, had great fun – the drifter couldn't get up to the ship, so we had to go in a super motorboat. It was grand.

Glad Uncle Bill went to Gainsborough, will drop a line sometime. Many thanks for Minnie's letter, it was very nice, and did I tell you I heard from Muriel? I will write soon, I have had a lot of mail recently, I'm afraid it will be coming to an end. Dorothy (Farrow) is coming on leave this week and she will try and come and see you. She is full of Tim, and I think it must be the real thing. He has gone to France, but she is hoping to be married in spring and would like me as bridesmaid!! Do you remember me saying any new frock I had was out of some stuff we had in? Well, Dorothy asks me (in fun) if we have "any stuff in" for a bridesmaid's dress. Ha!Ha!

Not a bit surprised about Audrey and George – are you sure it's not a wedding? However, I hope all goes well and they will be happy.

Mum, don't do anything about selling my bike, I have been

67

thinking I will wait until I can get another because I want one of some sort, it's just that I want a lighter one.

I went to see a good film: "English Without Tears". It was very very funny but with it there was a very good film about London, with some lovely scenes. You would have loved it.

I wonder if you have ever seen a rainbow caused by the moon! We saw one the other night at 2am. It was raining and in the distance across the sea was a strange pale quarter circle in the sky. It is the first time I have ever seen one.

I have just had my second supper – two fishcakes.

The newspapers are much appreciated, I have not read them yet but did just notice that Mabel Norton is dead. Did you know her?

Well, my dears, I have given you your 2½d worth this time, so will leave you and go to sleep.

Very much love,

Mary

Xxxxxxxx

xxxxxxxx

8

Into Autumn

"Your tatties are doing all right then," says Billy Craigie, "they've no' got the blight." Stopped in the middle of the road for a conversation, I patted Nouska the Samoyed through the car window. I'd seen Billy planting his well-chitted tatties a couple of weeks before I'd even bought mine. "Yes," he sighed, "they're looking good. Mine are all oot now, the blight finished them off. I think it's a bit more damp down here, ye ken." I commiserated, with only a slight touch of *schadenfreude* and breathed a sigh of relief that my tatties are okay, and in late August, are flowering.

By now the hectic wildlife carryings-on are calming down; the seabirds have departed, leaving only the fulmars and their oversized chicks, sitting like aged crones in frilly tutus on the ledges, watching the world go by. On my walks round the block, there are no longer any oystercatchers warning me off and only the odd curlew drifts across the wet fields. The winter migrants haven't arrived yet, apart from small groups of geese, and it's quiet: too quiet, as they say in the westerns. It's definitely autumnal. In Orkney, they say the summer ends with the agricultural shows in August.

One Sunday, I joined the Orkney Ramblers for a walk to the highest hill on Orkney Mainland, Ward Hill, a veritable peak at 269m. We started off by crossing the clay pigeon shoot, where no 'pigeons' were being shot; that would start later on. The site was a mess, with lots of plastic rubbish – from the cartridges, I suppose – and a few dead clay pigeons. Following the leader, we trudged up the slope, knee-deep in tussocky grass and heather. Mutiny broke out. "Why are we going this way?" came the protest. "There's a path just over there." Some even turned back!! Not showing much staying power, I thought, as I battled on with the more hardy elements; look on it as a work-out, we said, good for the thigh muscles. The view from the top was panoramic, if not spectacular, stretching north over the whole of West Mainland, even to my house, and south to Hoy. They're a nice crowd of people and we chatted over a picnic. Doug, the leader for the day, sighed: "You can plan a really scenic route, and wait for them to gasp at the view, but they're too busy chatting to notice."

"It's more a picnic club than a walking group," laughed one woman, "our lunch spots are always important."

Marion, a newly retired teacher, is fostering three ginger kittens and tried to persuade me to take them on. "But what about when I go away?" I argued.

"They can come to me," said another Sue, "I've already got eight cats." So far, I've managed to resist the temptation, not wanting to put the populations of Orkney voles, curlews and other ground-nesting birds under any more pressure than they are already. The biggest threat is from stoats, which were accidentally imported a few years ago, probably in animal feed or bedding, and have spread like a plague through this hitherto stoat-free paradise. Small mammal fans may well be happy, but local naturalists are definitely not: more stoats → fewer voles→ fewer hen harriers and short-eared owls, which are the native predators. Not to mention the effect on the other birds, all of which are ground-nesting: the curlews, lapwings, oystercatchers, snipe and skylarks. Meanwhile, Scottish Natural Heritage, whose job it is to look after this sort of thing, have been sitting on their hands and merely recording sightings. An excellent if unplanned research project, someone could even get a PhD for it. By the time they decide a stoat-cull is needed, it could be too late.[12]

In the continuing saga of my new boiler (the not-an-aga saga), I arrange for Magnus Fairpipe to come and fit it and the wood stove while I'm away south. First there's the question of a hearthstone, so I visit Geordie at the quarry up the road to Quoyloo. Initially he looks at me suspiciously, a bit wary, but warms up when I tell him where I live, especially as I say it's the place they call 'Squints'. A friend who's staying with me at the time admires a planter that he's made, an unusual sort of jigsaw of stone. We agree on a size and price and arrange for me to come back the next week. When I go back, it's not ready; it has split, so he's going to make another. I go home with a turnip and a bag of freshly dug potatoes instead. It's too heavy for me anyway, so Mr Fairpipe will pick it up when he fits the stove.

---

12   In late 2019 the Orkney Native Wildlife Project began trapping stoats with a view to eradication.

The next time I go is to pay for it. This time I'm in for a cup of tea and a piece of home-bake. His wife talks about her holiday – she likes to travel, he doesn't, but she's very chatty. Their son comes in who works on the Northern Isles ferry, and another friend, and there's a lot of banter, gossip about neighbours that I still can't absolutely understand. On the table, four slate place mats, one of which has the most beautiful, perfect fish fossil in it. Geordie made them; I'm dead impressed, but he just shrugs. "You chust don't know what you're going to find inside till you cut open the rock," he says.

Late September, and I'm back from 'sooth' after a laser follow-up to my cataract surgery and a visit to Ireland. Misty spider-webbed mornings. Indian summer sunny days.

Barony Mill is closed to visitors now that the harvest is in and I'm out of a job. I missed the 'thank you to volunteers' buffet lunch, so Rae Miller and his wife Margaret took me out for lunch at the Merkister Hotel and presented me with a certificate and Barony Mill mug. I got the best of that deal, the Merkister providing a much more upmarket *cullen skink* than the Birsay Community Hall.

Now the mill is closed, Rae has started milling the bere. I thought I'd better see for myself how it's done, so one morning got a text message: *I will be grapping from about 10.00 and grinding from around 12.00. Remember to wear your oldest and dirtiest clothes if you come.*

The first stage of the milling process involves de-husking the bere, done using the shilling stones. These are precisely adjusted so that only the husk is taken off and the grain stays whole. The mixture goes past a fanner and the husks, now called *scrubs*, are blown into a box while the heavier kernel of the grain is scooped up by an elevator and taken back to the top to drop down on the stones for the next stage. This process is grapping, which means crushing the de-husked bere into *grap*, rough oatmeal-size stuff; the very hard stones do this job, the French burrs. Lastly, grinding with the beremeal stone produces the final product, the fine, flour-like beremeal.[13]

Before all that, though, the grain has to be dried, spread out on the steel mesh kiln floor at the top of the building. The fire on the ground floor is stoked up and the heat rises up, passing through the grain and creating steam worthy of a steam room at a health spa. But what do you use for fire, you might be wondering. The beautifully sustainable answer is scrubs; one tonne of grain yields enough scrubs to dry the next tonne of grain. What miraculous organisation! The entire process, powered by water and waste product, is an exemplary model of sustainability and the use of renewable resources, and has been going since 1873.

So, on this September day, duly clad in my gardening jeans (naturally ripped) and old shirt, I turned up at around midday. I was later than intended, having been for an early swim with the Orkney Polar Bears, ending up shaking and teeth chattering for a couple of hours afterwards. In my defence, one of my fellow 'bears' was in a wetsuit and the other was

---

13   For milling bere there are three different stages using three types of millstone, unlike grinding wheat or oats, which only require two stages.

endowed with plenty of natural insulation colloquially referred to as 'bioprene'. I only got cold later on the drive home. It brought to mind that old cartoon:

Baby polar bear: Am I really a polar bear?
Mother polar bear: Yes, of course you are, why?
Baby polar bear: I'm f-f-f-freezing.

The water was pouring over the wheel at five times the rate we have it going for show purposes, and the grain was inching down the hopper to be trickled between the stones. The finished product, the beremeal, is shaken through sieves, and drips into a sack downstairs. Milling is not an occupation that's good for the lungs. The miller scoffs at the idea of wearing a dust mask but, as the grinding starts in earnest, one of the committee members who is helping dons one, with overalls. The dust must be there but is still so fine so as to be seen only when the door opens and a beam of light illuminates the flecks of 'stour'. I'm given the job of weighing out 1.5kg of the newly milled beremeal into brown paper bags. The weighing is easy, but the bag tops have to be folded over and sewn up by a machine that seems to have a mind of its own. I pull the trigger and the machine runs away with itself, leaving an escaping line of stitches independent of the flap. I'm soon relieved of the responsibility, in the kindest possible way. It will take a bit of practice before I master the technique.

Another task waiting for my return from 'sooth' was the potato harvest. A couple of weeks of dry weather seemed a propitious time to start, and the haulms (known locally as shas) were dying down. The tatties were good, and only a few had little worms in. Over the next couple of weeks, I managed to get them all out, only stopped by rain once. Should I leave them in longer – better storage facilities in the ground, after all – or get them out, away from the ravages of slugs and little eelworms? Out was my answer, the worms being apparently more common in the wetter parts of the plot. So, not wanting to miss the drier weather, I got them all out, carefully sorting the damaged ones for quick use and packing the sound ones in sacks for storage in a wardrobe in the garage.

I had a great crop, probably enough to last me for three years at an average rate of tattie-eating, so, very proud of my achievements, I gave bags of potatoes to friends and neighbours.

October

It really is an Indian summer, and there are some uncannily calm days. The sunrises, now at a sensible time of the morning, are spectacular; sun lifts over Birsay moors, tipping over and goldenly spilling across the fields, picking out fences, the spikes and tussocks of grass making long shadows. The Firth at Finstown is not bestirred by the merest ripple. The lochs of Harray and Stenness spread out like white silk. Scapa Flow seems to be barely flowing, the sea solidified. The hills are darkly sharp silhouetted cardboard cutouts against a lucent sky and fade to a misty base floating above the fields. All shades of green are there, apple to sage, to mint to olive, interspersed with barley or oat gold. The moors are a rusty, reddish brown with the red grasses, and faded smudgy beige-pink heather.

One Sunday morning, I'm roused from deep sleep by cows mooing, very loud and close. I try to ignore them but eventually have to get up. Farmer Arty is in the road stopping the traffic, what little there is on a Sunday morning in rural Orkney, and cows are crossing. It's only later in the day when I found hoof marks on the lawn that I realise the cows must have been *very* close, and what were they doing, trampling around my garden? Later in the week, chatting with Moira, she asks if I'd seen cows in the road. "I heard the kye bogling," she said, "and looked oot that way but I didna see anything." Bogling! "Yes," she said, "that's what we say for mooing."

Hundreds of starlings line the wires. On a quiet sunny morning, they sit and preen, fluffing up the feathers, shaking and scratching, wiping the beaks as though sharpening them. Or they may be on the roof, then peel off in formation, a squadron of fighter jets. In the evenings, they swarm in clouds, whirling in mobius designs. Further along the wires, there are tinier birds, hundreds of what I think are twite.

A ringtail hen harrier makes a low fly-past over the thistles in the back garden, vole-hunting. In the next field, something has died. A black-backed gull and a hooded crow are arguing about the carcass, and the gull is winning. Beside the crow, none too small itself, the black-back is monstrous, shooing the hoodie away with a slight forward sally if it gets a little too close, and the hoodie jumps back. Later, a black cat takes over the job of scavenging, and later still, a raven.

Another Sunday, there's a walk with the Ramblers on Graemsay, a small island between Stromness and Hoy. We take the ferry across, and the plan is to walk around the island. It's so terribly calm there are midges, the first time I've ever noticed them in Orkney. The lunch spot for this walk is an abandoned church, taken over by a local farmer as a store for machinery and, having suffered the usual incursion by farm animals, is in a bit of a mess. Further round the coast, at the west end of the island, we reach the small lighthouse of Hoy Low, and old gun emplacements. A chimneystack is all that remains of the officers' house. It's sunny and, yes, *warm*, and I long for a swim. There's a very special beach made entirely of seashells, a *maerl* beach. It's gorgeous. We wander about and play with the shells, poke around the rock pools, or sit and have another swig of tea.

Predictably, the calm doesn't last. Another day, bright, with a gale force wind. Only me at Marwick Head, and I keep away from the cliff edge.

As the wind increases, there is a flurry of activity from the birds. An explosion of light gull feathers, turbulent as a shaken snowdome against the dark green. Migrants are arriving. Lines of geese score by, stitching the sky; the lochs are pocked with ducks. Some are escaping from the northern winter and will just rest up here a while, and others stay here all winter. The fields are full of them. The grass-guzzling greylag geese are not welcomed by farmers, and the shooters are out. Sometimes there's a pop in the still air and you see then men with guns. Meanwhile, the news is full of other migrants, human refugees, heading towards the northern winter, fleeing threats worse than cold, but still not welcomed by frightened governments.

The wind has opened a crack in the clouds; the sky is a wonder of celestial peach and soft fulmar-feather grey, low light picking out every field, ditch, wall and fence. It amazes me.

Here, the dark is shockingly dark. After months of sleeping through the crazily short nights, now it's dark by 6.30pm. There's some deep and spacy hollow quality about it, a thrill of driving through the blackness picked out with a few house lights.

Walking back from Dounby one day, I call in on Billy Craigie and his wife Norma. Their house is called Benzieclett, which means, they tell me, 'Near the burn called the Clett'. They built it themselves when they were first married, while they were staying at Bryameadow, a little way up the road from me. And when they say they built it themselves, they mean it: "We even made wor own blocks." Norma hasn't moved far in her life. She was born in Sandwick and this house where we're sitting is built on the site of her grandmother's house, where she spent a lot of time. "And you know," she says, "the land's getting lower. I know it is because when I was a girl an' I wanted to see if me mither was home yet, I'd have to walk up the brae to see if she was at the hoose, but now, ye can jes see it clear from here."

Leaving their house, I glance down at my cosy new fleece-lined black trousers: Nouska the Samoyed has left me a generous free gift of lovely white fur.

Round the corner, I meet a woman coming out of the house with a bucket, a window swisher, a woolly hat and a cute round bespectacled face. Putting the bucket down, she stops for a chat: no hurry in Orkney. She doesn't like the salt spray on her windows and the recent wind has added plenty of that. After establishing that it's not a bad day after yesterday and weren't we lucky this month, we had so many bonny days, we get on to more important stuff. Who am I, where do I stay,[14] where have I come from and why. Am I the wan that stays by Moira and Chockie? Ah. She's heard about me. Moira and Chockie are her daughter's in-laws, the daughter and husband (M and Ch's son) live just up there – nodding to a house a couple of hundred yards up the road – with Paul, he's the one that works for the Hydro, that used to work for Merrimans, with the van and James. Round here, it's a good place to live, she says. Everybody looks out for you, you know what everyone's doing! With this in mind, I'm very open about what my plans are, where I'm going. The talk turns to animals – have I got any – and my field.

Bob and Mymie used to keep geese, fatten them up for Christmas, but of course, you can't do that if you're going away. And next year Jimmy (her husband) might be able to help with cutting my grass. He has a finger mower. Mairi and Jimmy Walls. "We'll see you before you go," she says, and turns to start washing the windows. Walking on, I wonder if she'll get more water because what she has in the bucket must undoubtedly be cold by now. I imagine a finger mower, neatly

---

14   In Orkney this means where do you *live*.

clipping off the ends of my fingers, all the better to fit into my gloves.

Hallowe'en is called Divilmint Night here. I was warned to take in my house sign, in case it 'goes for a walk'. There were dire stories of the old days, of farm trailers being moved mysteriously to appear the next day, twenty of them all neatly parked in the car park at Dounby School. Gates might be removed and found several miles away, and – more mundane but equally annoying – houses and shops may be splattered with flour and water. I took my sign in. On the 1st of November, sure enough, the proprietor of a local craft shop was to be seen furiously washing the flour paste from her windows.

Pumpkins costing between £1.50 and £2.50 before Hallowe'en are reduced to 10p; good for those who only want it for soup or Americans who want it for Thanksgiving pie making, or anyone who isn't worried about having their lantern on the correct night. These are a fairly recent introduction, and one of the friendly receptionists at the swimming pool doesn't like them. "They're fairly wrong," she says ('fairly' in Orkney meaning *completely*!), "we always used to make a 'pop' (a lantern) out of a neep, and we used to take it round on bonfire night and ask for a 'penny for my pop'."

Out for a walk one day, I get a text message from Rae: *Have you eaten hare?* He's cooked far too much, and I'm invited to help eat it. I'm torn. *Isn't hare a bit too cute?* I ask.

Not cute at all, they're vermin, comes the reply, *especially when they eat your vegetables.* I'd planned to go for a swim, but the pool will still be there, and it's not polite to turn down an invitation. It was *very* good, washed down with a glass of his home brew beer made from malted bere.

9

November

Wren Tel L.M.Walker 94167
WRNS Quarters
Haybrake
Lyness
Orkney
3/11/1944

My dearest Mum and all,

This letter comes to you from Cabin 5, and I am writing it in bed, so please forgive any scrawl that is worse than usual because I am as far down the blankets as possible.

Well, how are you all? I expect I shall be having a letter sometime. I hope Uncle Bill's glasses are mended because I haven't heard from any of you this week. Don't let Dad strain his eyes writing until he is really well. I had a most vivid dream about him last night, we were looking at his left eye.

Nothing very exciting has happened but there always seems to be something interesting to see and do and never have I known time fly so rapidly. It seems to go at a frightening speed and in thirty days' time I'll be home with you once more – don't get excited and don't make any special preparations – but I do want you, Mum, to rest as much as possible before I do come. The Boys must make you rest – don't forget, Boys.

I believe I told you that Betty and I went for a lovely walk on Sunday. We followed the coast road north-east for several miles. The scenery was very lovely indeed with the wild grandeur of Bamford Edge and Burbage, yet much more lovely, really, because of the sea and all the little islands and bays; the islands in the distance were golden and shimmering in the sunshine and never have I seen such wonderful colourings of sea and sky and hills. Any artist who had been with us on Sunday afternoon would have gone completely nutty. The hills were all different shades – many of them brown and gold and green – so that from a distance they almost looked camouflaged with the rusty bracken and faded heather intermingled with vivid grass and mosses. The gulls and gannets screamed and wheeled over the little bays and creeks, the sea lapped very gently on the mossy stones below us and we felt as we walked back to an eagerly awaited supper that we were glad to be here, in spite of the fact that we have to put up with so many trivial inconveniences.

After supper, we went to church and thoroughly enjoyed the service. We go very rarely because we are not often off duty on a Sunday, and the first time I did not enjoy the service, but it was very good on Sunday night. The chaplain was a sandy-haired Scot – rather dour, but with a strong suspicion of a twinkle in his eye and a very able preacher.

We were celebrating Halloween this week and had a party with pukka turnip lanterns, and it was great fun.

Betty and I were dancing last night again, this time at an army dance, and had a lot of good fun and good eats, although with about four strides one could go twice down the hall it was so tiny.

(I can hear a mouse scratching at the floor behind my bed, it is a very irritating sound.)

Give my love to anybody I haven't written to, it's a heck of a job keeping up with correspondence, but I am doing my best.

I'll have to get up now and go on duty, so will leave you for a day or two.

All my love,
Tons of it,
Mary
Xxxxxxxxxxxxxxxxx
Xxxxxxxxxxxxxxxxxx

Wren Tel L.M.Walker 94167
WRNS Quarters
Haybrake
RN Base
Lyness
Orkney
12/11/44

Dearest Mum and all,

Another week gone by as swiftly as all the others and now three weeks today I will be leaving for my leave and 5pm on the 4th of Dec will be arriving at Sheffield Victoria station. I had intended springing it on you for a surprise, but I had to tell you just when I should be arriving so that if my little pie-faced chicken has his old bus around that area we will be able to proceed to dear old "Pengwern". If, however, ye olde coach is out of action through lack of juice, etc., I will take one of Mr Reuben Thompson's cars and arrive at number 54 about 5.30pm for a delicious tea where, if the lady of the house is well, we will have new flat cakes and butter and cold roast beef and fried potatoes followed by more flat cakes and cheese and HP sauce (no bread to be specially baked unless Lady of the House is on specially super form).

I never wrote to Gainsboro, have you heard from them lately? If not, please remind them that I am coming home, and they will need to kill the pig earlier than usual. This is <u>very important</u> as I shall literally die if I don't have pig for Christmas – <u>please note this</u>. Thanks.

It is Sunday pm and I am lying in bed having just had a bath and washed my hair. We had a good dinner today (most unusual) of pork and apple sauce and peas and baked potatoes and prunes, apricots, etc. Am going on duty at 8pm, so am just scrawling these few lines, although I have nothing to say.

I have written to America to Muriel and Cousin Minnie and sent them both Christmas cards too – aren't I good?

Have you been keeping okay, Dad? I do hope you are heaps better and can see better too and Mum, you are resting.

Nothing more to say ducks.

Tons and tons of love,

Mary xxxx

Only a month to go till the shortest day, and the first snow lies powdered over the Birsay Moors to the east and the Hoy Hills to the south. I'm walking south on the cliffs from Yesnaby and then turn inland. Little pockets of frozen hail are still there in hollows by mid-afternoon, and in the golden reedy grass by the Burn of Uppadee I disturb a snipe: only a metre in front of me and still I don't see it. It explodes out of its cover and zig zags erratically away, confounding predators. Over the peaty, boggy, mossy watershed, a female hen harrier patrols along the side of the burn and disappears round the shoulder of the hill called the Face of Scarra. At this point, only 3-4km separate the Loch of Stenness from the sea, and these hills form the rim of the saucer that is West Mainland Orkney. In the middle of the saucer are the lochs, and other marshy pockets are increasingly waterlogged. The place is becoming a central wetland.

November, my first winter, and I've been blessed with an Indian summer that extended into late autumn. Everyone agrees we deserve it, after the rubbish summer, and it'll make the winter seem shorter. In the afternoon dusk, a short-eared owl, locally called 'cattie face', quarters my back garden, hovering moth-like in search of voles. On a calm, clear night, the geese can be heard gaggling on the flooded fields, or a lone late curlew calls. It's a pity about the lights of Dounby a couple of miles away, but even so, the sky is spectacularly dark; enough to see the Milky Way, and layers and layers of stars. On stormy nights, the wind drowns out most of the bird sounds and batters at the windows, tearing away at the 'windsock' tea towel. There've been few of those nights, but the wind doesn't get in; my house is cosy. One evening, after checking out the Orkney Aurora Group Facebook page, we dashed to the car and headed for the north coast at Birsay, aurora borealis chasing. The car was gently buffeted by a fresh south-west wind, the Brough of Birsay lighthouse beamed on our left, and north over the sea to Westray, was the Noup Head light. Matthew saw more shooting stars than he'd seen in his life; the non-shooting ones hung there, glittering and flashing in the wind, whilst in the north, this green glow was, indeed, the Northern Lights. Not quite the drama that I'd expected but definitely there, and enthralling. Some people stay out all night, aurora watching and waiting. The German neighbour of a friend "would sit all night in his chair with his flask and his blanket". There can be traffic jams after midnight on the single-track road past the Ring of Brodgar, keen photographers wanting to get that iconic shot of the standing stones with aurora. My optimistic image of the aurora borealis, apart from photographs, had been largely based on scenes from my favourite film, *Local Hero*, the one where Mac screams down the phone line from a red telephone booth in Aberdeenshire to Houston, Texas: *"Now it's red all over!"*; I've yet to see it red all over. The Facebookers post surreal pictures taken with long exposures gathering all the possible light, showing rays and arcs and curtains. They discuss the cameras, lenses, exposures, apertures and times. It all seems a bit deceptive and unreal to me and I want to see the Merry Dancers dancing with my naked eyes. So, I wait and am rewarded later in the year with green celestial searchlights moving over the Firth at Finstown as I drive to get the night ferry.

On Guy Fawkes Night, there was a huge bonfire, the biggest I've ever seen, piled with pallets, high as a tower block of flats. Marshalls shooed people round to one side, for when it was lit, the flames would be blown in the very direction where folk were arriving. Attempting to keep alive the old tradition of 'pops', the community council had instituted a 'pop' competition; a dozen children paraded along with their turnip lanterns, which were later thrown into the fire. Sure enough, the flames were blown almost horizontal, making magical shapes, evoking that ancient awe and mystery of fire. As a scientist, I know something about what a flame is; still, trying to watch the passage of flame from where it starts to where it disappears evokes fear and wonder. If the wind swings round now, we'll all be singed. It doesn't, though. There's a gentle atmosphere, no wild behaviour and, after the fireworks, we disperse in a safe, calm and orderly Orkney manner.

By the end of the month, the weather has taken a dramatic turn. On the low cliffs of the coast north of the Bay of Skaill, the sea-spray is scooped up and deposited violently against the salt-burnt brown and sodden grass. The blackest clouds I've ever seen turn out to be full of hail, which batters the windows and rushes in horizontal waves over the fields. Two minutes later, there's a hole in the blackness, full of bright blue sky and glorious piles of brilliant white cumulus clouds.

Yes, the weather is a major character in Orkney life: the others, all around me, are the Orcadians who've been so welcoming and friendly to a 'ferry-looper' as we non-natives are known.

There's Euan, the car body man who, after sucking in through his teeth and tutting, has agreed to fit a new door to my car. Leaving for the ferry in the 5.30am dark, I'd misjudged the position of the wall and given the passenger door a thorough scraping. Euan tells a good tale. As a teenager, he had a friend who worked at the Crantit Cheese factory. There were great big steel tanks they used to make the cheese in, and while 'washing out the tanks', the friend would fill them up with water, heat it up, and they would all get in and have a swim. "Nothing better, on a cold day," he said, "and, of course, in those days we had no electricity at home, no bath or running water. We cleaned it all out before they made the next batch of cheese," he added hastily, "and anyway, the place is closed down now."

Another story was of the Great Salmon Escape, which featured salmon breaking out of the fish farm. The bay was full of them, folk were scooping them up in their hands. "They told us not to eat them, they said they might be toxic, but nobody took any notice. Everyone's freezers were full of salmon."

The talk, as ever, turns to the wind, once more on the increase. He tells me how Orkney used to be egg supplier to the nation, especially during WWII. I knew from Mum's letters that the troops would send eggs home but hadn't any idea how big the business was: 7,000 hen houses, 73 million eggs per year. Orkney's main export business. This was interrupted in 1952 when a hurricane blew away the hen houses complete with 86 thousand hens. Some of the wooden hencoops were seen floating in the sound between Rousay and West Mainland, heading north. All was not lost, however, or rather, some were quickly replaced; folk from the rest of Britain rallied round, and point of lay hens were sent north from all over the country. Egg production peaked in the late fifties but the advent of large-scale production in mainland Scotland meant that the number of eggs exported from Orkney declined. Fortunately for me, there are still plenty of backyard hens and honesty egg boxes, from where I buy really fresh eggs with bright yellow yolks.

"You'll like the wind, though," says Euan, "that's why Orkney folk are so bent over and peedie.[15] You should go over to the Ness and watch when the Hamnavoe's[16] going past, that'll be a sight for you, if she's not cancelled o'course." He tells how once he'd spotted his wife getting out of the car and expected her through the house door any minute, but she didn't come, and she didn't come, so he had to go out and look for her. "There she was, pinned against the wall. She couldn't cross the gap between the garage and the hoose for the wind."

Now the tourists have gone, the community life of Orkney really takes off. In the summer, they're all too busy gardening, I'm told. There are amateur dramatic groups, choirs, evening classes, traditional dancing and music, yoga, films and talks on a huge range of topics: from dragonflies to ultra-marathons, from women in the Hudson's Bay company to plans for the eradication of invasive stoats.

Up the road, at the house that used to be the Twatt post office, there appears a sign:

I ♥ Twatt

And on the other side:

---

15 Peedie = small.
16 The Hamnavoe is the ferry which plies between Stromness and Scrabster on the Scottish mainland. It's also the old name for the port of Stromness.

The hamlet of
TWATT.
Now twinned with
Nuneaton

What can I say?!

It's getting colder. One morning I looked out and the grass was a funny colour. No wind. To my amazement, it was frosty! The cold weather gives me chilblains – well, a chilblain to be exact, on the same toe that in Tanzania last year had a jigger in it. I'm beset by worry: is it really a chilblain, or is it jigger's eggs hatched out and making my skin near the toenail itchy and swollen? Those among you who are aficionados of cocktail making will know that a jigger is some sort of vessel for mixing cocktails. This is not that sort of jigger. This jigger is a parasitic sand flea that jumps on to a bare foot, burrows into the skin and lays eggs. The eggs hatch out and feed on the flesh. Euuk! I've acquired two separate ones in my time in Africa and both were got out before they did any damage. Hydrogen peroxide is put into the wound to kill any eggs that may have already been laid. My worry was that the second time, the thing was dug out at home, without the benefit of hydrogen peroxide. So, what if it had laid its eggs?? Or maybe part of its body remained there, and it had gone putrid? I can make up all sorts of horrible health scenarios in the dead of night. I plastered it with antiseptic cream and hoped for the best.

The groups are all planning their Christmas meals but due to bad timing I won't be here to participate as I'm leaving tomorrow for Tanzania (and my *soi-disant* love): Christmas by the Indian Ocean seems a good idea.

★ ★ ★

Mum was leaving Orkney to go on leave in Sheffield, arriving on the 4th of December – I'm leaving on the same date to go to Tanzania. At sixty-five years of age, *her* mother was waiting at home for the return of her beloved only daughter, being exhorted to rest as much as possible. I'm off, only slightly younger, on my travels again with no intention of resting.

I imagine my mother, cuddled down in the blankets in Cabin 5. It must have been freezing. Blankets! Before the days of duvets and central heating, they were far tougher than we are now. Before the days of fleeces and Gore-Tex waterproofs.

My Mum, Mary Walker, was excited at the adventure of being in Orkney and having a good life with friends, but also longing for home; love shines through her letters with a warmth that makes me feel – what – guilty? Envious? It might seem a stupid question, they were her parents after all, but what made her love home so much? I loved my parents and had a wonderful secure and loving childhood, but for me at her age, twenty-four, there was always that impatience and longing for escape that I never failed to act on. Was it their vulnerability, or was she simply, at the same age, a much much nicer, less selfish person than me? I came to the reluctant and uncomfortable conclusion that yes, she was.

10

Preparing for Christmas

Wren Tel L.M.Walker 94167
WRNS Quarters
Haybrake
Lyness
Orkney
19ᵗʰ Nov

My dearest Mum, Dad and "Joe", [17]

It is Sunday morning and I have just come back from Kirkwall, having stayed the night in the Wrennery there.

I received your super letters just now. They are so lovely and cheerful and interesting, you old ducks. I have bought the most lovely length of tweed for a coat. I am having it sent and by now you will have received it. I bought three and a quarter yards to be on the safe side – I am sure you will love it. It is a glorious shade in the daylight, and I shall be able to wear anything with it. I shall just have a plain tailored coat made; it is a beautiful tweed, as you will see, and we could not buy anything like it in Sheffield. I have

---

17   Joseph William Wilkinson, her Uncle Bill. Not Joe her boyfriend from before the war who didn't want them to be committed to each other. He was almost always referred to as Uncle Bill, but occasionally 'Joe' as a bit of fun.

not got the lining, but we will get it at home. The tweed cost me £4, which is remarkably cheap considering the quality, and I am longing to know what you think of it. I shall be able to wear it on Easter Sunday. Oh Boy.

Mum, I will get you some when I come back from leave, if you like, and will bring some samples with me when I come.

As regards the other things, presents and so on, I haven't been able to get very much – I want to buy something from Scotland for Brenda but could not find anything yesterday, but one of the girls is going over this week to try to find a wee tartan purse or something similar for me. I have bought a pair of stockings for Auntie Ada and am going to buy nice toilet soap in Edinburgh for Auntie Edith and Cousin Edith as I can't think of anything else; also, any last minute things I want. We shall have about an hour and a half in Edinburgh and Betty's mother is going to meet us with tea and sandwiches so that we shan't have to waste time having a meal and we will be able to have a quick look at Princes Street. I shall not cart a lot of baggage around but will only bring the essentials. I will take my small case back with me and when I come back to Lyness will buy a light service suitcase from the stores – it will be much better than the one I have and the naval issue are very good.

We had a really lovely weekend – at least, when I say weekend, I mean a day. Yesterday we came off duty at 8am feeling rather sleepy but we rushed around, had breakfast and tidied up our cabins and ourselves, packing our pyjamas and toothbrushes, etc. (we had a sleeping out pass to go to Kirkwall). We hurried down to the pier to catch the 10.30 drifter. Betty and I and Margaret and Audrey, all on the same watch, were going. It was lovely – we were indeed lucky after the wintry weather of the past week and it was a very pleasant trip, *particularly as it was a large drifter, so we had shelter. We arrived in good time and went straight to lunch, very nice too and we were ready for it. The wind was so icy our cheeks burned and our feet were frozen, but we soon thawed out over a lovely fire in the small café where we always go, and after lunch we started to do our shopping. I bought Auntie Rose a Scottish calendar, very lovely Scottish scenes, which I think she will like. I have not bought owt for Phyllis, but I want to get something before I come home. Can you suggest anything I could get in Edinburgh for her? I have not bought presents for Joan, Ray or Dorothy yet, but will do so when I arrive home.*

After we had done quite a bit of shopping we thought it was time we had some tea, so we went up to the Church of Scotland canteen – it is a splendid place, far better than ours in Lyness – and we had poached egg on toast and scones, very nice too. Afterwards, we should have done more shopping, but we decided to deposit our things at the Wrennery and find it before dark. It was a much better place by far than these quarters, much more comfortable and cheerful and clean. All four of us were in the same cabin and, armed with sheet and blankets, we went to make our beds. Everything was so different from ours and so warm. We even had plugs in the basins, which is more than we have here. We decided that, as it was now about 6pm, we would have supper there, so we went down to the mess where we had a meal of steamed whiting (or fresh haddock) and jam and butter and coffee. It was so nicely served up too and the mess was very clean and newly decorated and modern.

We wanted to go somewhere but did not want to see the one picture which was on, so decided to see Dobson and Young again (they had come over on our drifter). We went to the cinema where they were appearing and saw half of the first performance of the film and then came out and went back to see *D & Y*. Although it was very similar to Tuesday night's lecture, it was very good, and we thoroughly enjoyed it. When we came out, we quickly made our way to the one and only fish and chip shop, which was something we had been trying to do ever since we came to the Orkneys. We discovered it eventually after winding our way along narrow dark streets of the little quaint town. We had hot sausage rolls and chips, which we ate on the way back. It was strange being in a town that is still completely blacked out and has not even 'starlighting';[18] it reminded me of the early days of the war. It was strange too to walk along streets in the darkness and to have high walls around you blocking out the sky; you see here it is all so open and one gets a feeling of endless space, you see the huts are all only one storey high and even the cottages are low roofed.

We were very tired when we got back to the cabin and could scarcely keep our eyes open, for we had been awake about thirty-six hours with the exception of a couple of hours before we went on duty. We went over to the galley for a cup of cocoa and then had a lovely hot bath and went off to bed. (The baths, I should add, are a terrific length and even <u>I</u> could lie down with six inches to spare – all right for Uncle Bill.)

Unfortunately, we had to be up early this morning as we were on duty at noon, and we had to catch the 8.30 drifter. We had a <u>boiled egg</u> for breakfast for the first time since we had been in the WRNS and thoroughly enjoyed it. We dashed off for our bus and had to wait about eighteen minutes for it. The streets were very quiet and deserted

---

18   Street lighting using low wattage bulbs. Blackout rules were gradually eased during 1940 because of large numbers of accidents in the dark, but the Dim-out, lights equivalent to moonlight, was only introduced in September 1944.

in the half light of early Sunday morning and there was an atmosphere of peace around the cathedral square, the only movement the clouds scudding across the grey November sky.

At last, the bus arrived, and we proceeded to the pier. The drifter was the same one we went in. It was cold and we were all rather sleepy, so were delighted when we found a tiny cabin, which had lovely cushions just big enough for the four of us to lie down, so we spent the rest of the trip there and we were soon back in Lyness. Now I am back at work and, being Sunday, it's pretty quiet. Tonight, I am going to try and phone you, so that's the end of my adventures for another week.

Uncle Bill, I think you must have misunderstood me, I <u>did</u> write to Arthur immediately – I only asked you if you'd told him I was in the Orkneys! Okay?

Well, dears, I haven't time to write any more now. I think this is enough to be going on with.

Heaps of love,
Mary

It is HMS Proserpine anyhow, ducks, not HMS Haybrake, that's only the quarters.

Dobson and Young, I discovered, were popular entertainers who gave lectures on music in a series called "Music with a Smile". They toured all over Britain and were responsible for introducing huge numbers of service personnel to the delights of classical music. Imagine going to a film and coming out halfway to go and see something else!

I wonder what happened to the tweed. Did she get the coat

made? Did she wear it at Easter? Her delight at the purchase is so touching, especially when you think of our throwaway fashions nowadays. That coat would have lasted well beyond the end of the war, during my childhood presumably. Although, of course, it might not have fitted her by then…

"Joe", by the way, and Uncle Bill, were one and the same person, my mum's uncle, the brother of her mother. Also referred to in the previous letter as "my little pie-faced chicken". What's that about, I wonder, did he like eating pies?

He lived with them in the house they moved to and rented during the war, 'Pengwern'. I was always told that Pengwern meant 'head of the valley' in Welsh, but Google translate now tells me 'gwern' means alder, as in the tree. Sure enough, there were loads of alder trees across the road alongside the River Porter. Uncle Bill was a travelling salesman for an engineering company, with (gasp!) a car – the one Mum calls an old bus. Pretty rare in those days, I should think.

Talking to my neighbours, Moira and Jackie, I mentioned the Wrennery, saying how Mum had liked Kirkwall and that the Wrens' quarters there were so much nicer than in Lyness.

"Well now," exclaims Moira, "we've got plasterboard from the Wrennery, there in the bedrooms!" When the building was being demolished in the late sixties, Orkney people, being island folk and not inclined to let anything go to waste, made use of any materials they could. Moira and Jackie were building their 'hoose' and went and salvaged enough plasterboard to line their bedrooms. "It was small pieces ye ken, that had to be stuck togither, an' a bit of green at the bottom, nice."

Wren Tel L.M.Walker 94167
Haybrake
Lyness
Orkney
21/12/44

My dearest Mum and all,

I have just received your letters and card, very many thanks. It was lovely to have your letter, Dad, and to know you could see so well to write to me and it was such an interesting letter, lots more please.

(Mum, while I remember, I never gave Mrs Jenkinson that 2/- that I owed her – will you do so please – thank you.)

It was grand to hear your voices again yesterday, I'm sorry the line was so bad. I could hear you very well, though. I do hope you keep better, Mum, and have as nice a Christmas as possible. I only wish I could be with you. We are having a party on Christmas Day, so if my frock doesn't arrive for Monday, I can wear it on New Year's Day.

I have already told you that we were held up in Thurso because of the gales – well, we had quite an interesting time and were very comfortable at the Wrennery and quite enjoyed ourselves. In the afternoon, we went for a walk, it was so sunny, and went down to the beach and watched the lovely white breakers and then walked round the quaint old deserted streets. Being Sunday, it was very very quiet. We decided we would have tea at one of the hotels, The Royal. The five of us trooped in and had afternoon tea in the lounge. At 5pm, we had high tea, delicious baked potatoes and bacon and sausage with toast, jam, etc., and thoroughly enjoyed it. Afterwards, we went to church, but it was a rather disappointing service with very very few people and lacked inspiration – I think we chose the wrong church, but it was dark when we went. However, we thoroughly enjoyed our "farewell to civilisation".

The next day was calm, and we had to get up very early and in great haste and it was still dark when we embarked. This time a different drifter. Rose and I stayed on deck but the others went to sleep. It was lovely to watch the sun rising and we had a pleasant trip, spending most of the time on the bridge with the skipper and the time passed very quickly.

We did not start working on Monday but on Tuesday afternoon. Betty was pleased to see me, and we had a lot to talk about before she went on Wednesday. I have already missed her a lot and am sorry she won't be here for Christmas.

We are very busy decorating the cabin and I have just been making paper chains. They look very pretty, and we have chains of pink and white paper and cotton wool festooned all over. We have also managed to get some holly but as yet no mistletoe, not that there will be any use for it (at any rate not in the <u>cabin</u>).

Today I have had a lovely parcel from Joan. She sent me a very nice, iced Christmas cake, complete with frill, and a very lovely box of hankies and a huge jar of cream. Have also had several cards, one from Muriel.

We were dancing last night, it was quite good, especially when the electricity failed, and we were dancing in the dark for about half an hour.

Well, dear, I must go to bed now. Very much love and a peaceful Xmas to you all.

Your loving Mary

11

The Festive Season

Wren Tel L.M.Walker
Haybrake
Lyness
Orkney
Xmas Eve 1944

My dear Mum and Dad and Uncle Bill,

It seems very unlike Christmas Eve here. We went on the morning watch, so slept until 2pm, and since then we have been 'canteening' and have collected about eight bars of chocolate from the various canteens.

I have just heard on the radio that V bombs have been launched against northern England and am very anxious to know if they have been anywhere near us. I'm afraid the whole of the news this week has made me feel very depressed. I do hope that when I do hear from you again, you'll have something cheerful to say to me.

Nothing in the least exciting has happened up here, nor seems likely to. Flo and Pat and I went to a carol service on Friday, which was very enjoyable, and yesterday, after sleeping most of the day, we went to the Base dance, which was the usual hectic scrum with many and varied types of men and which wasn't very exciting.

The cabin here looks very pretty – we have pinky white chains and holly and candles, which look very nice at night.

26ᵗʰ

It is now Boxing Day and I have been working all morning and go on at 8pm again. On Christmas Eve, we went to carol singing at the Church of Scotland and then feasted in the cabin on Spam and pears and cream (which Flo had brought) and Christmas cake. At 10pm we all got ready to go to the midnight service. It was held at the Base Church, which is a large Nissen hut very like a church and holding about 500 people. There was a Christmas tree lit by many fairy lights and reaching almost to the ceiling near to the altar. It is rather high church, with a great deal of ceremony, but I thoroughly enjoyed the service, which was very impressive. The church was very full, packed with many different types of people, captains, commanders, army colonels, Wren officers, dockworkers and, of course, ordinary ratings. I took communion, as did most of the people, and it was the first time I have done so in C of E. We eventually went to bed about 1.30am but could fortunately lie in the next day. On Christmas Day we had a very marvellous dinner, served up by the officers. There was tomato soup, roast turkey, baked potatoes, turnips and peas, bread sauce, etc. and plum pud with rum sauce and nuts, dates, oranges and apples. It was very pleasant to be waited on for a change, but today we have gone back to the same old routine, worse luck.

Unfortunately, we had to work in the afternoon, and the last dog until 8pm. We had a very good tea with ham and pork and all manner of cakes, trifle, etc. After we came from duty we went to the dance, which was held in the recreation rooms (my frock didn't arrive, Mum, so I went in uniform). Before we went to the dance, I put on my very best stockings and tripped over the mat in the corridor and ruined them. I was furious!!

The dance was absolutely packed to suffocation point, all the Wrens and about three times as many men, the majority of whom – in fact 99½% of them – were quite quite "merry". Never in the whole of my life have I seen anything to equal it and I can't say that I really thoroughly enjoyed it. I can't think what the New Year will be like – certainly can't be any worse than last night.

Many thanks for the calendar, Uncle Bill, I received today, and a card from Miss Hensman and a hanky, which had obviously been used and washed – not too clean, either.

Forgive this appalling writing but I am sitting up in bed, it's cold and there's no heating on today.

I hope I'll have a letter from you today. Hope you had a nice day yesterday – I thought about you the whole day. I hope I'll be home next Christmas.

Lots of love,
Mary
PS Parcel just arrived.
Thanks very much, Mum dear.

Wren Tel L.M.Walker
Haybrake
Lyness
1ˢᵗ Jan 1945

My dear Mum and all,

Today I have begun the New Year well by writing two letters, one to Mr Chandler and one to Mr Clarke, Brunswick, both of which have been hanging fire for a long time. Most of the day I spent in bed having come off the morning watch at 8am feeling very tired after the dance last night.

103

We had a New Year dance in the quarters, which was quite good, and in the traditional Scots fashion complete with eightsome reels and pipers and quite a few people had a wee bottle tucked away somewhere ready to celebrate the New Year, and quite a few people had already had a drop but it was not as bad, in that respect, as the Christmas one. At midnight they sounded sixteen bells, and we all sang Auld Lang Syne and there was a great deal of kissing. One just kissed anyone and everyone, which was very very funny. My partner was a pleasant Scotsman, but he unfortunately hadn't his little bottle, but perhaps it was just as well.

As we went back to the cabin, all the ships in the harbours were sounding their sirens and hooters and the sky was lit with 'faery' lights and rockets, it was quite thrilling, and the hooting went on for a long time, it was rather eerie. We went on watch at 2am feeling rather weary and some of the men were certainly slightly the worse for wear. We had a tot given to us but have not been able to drink it yet.

I'll have to stop now because it's suddenly busy.

Heaps of love and Happy New Year!!!
Mary

Wren Tel L.M.Walker
Haybrake
Lyness
Orkney
16th Jan

My dearest Mum and all,
I received your letter last night, it was really lovely and long and such a lot of news. I'm so glad you are feeling better and that you are

getting some help. I'm afraid it is almost impossible for me to tell you when I am ringing up, but I will phone again in about two weeks' time, but don't stop in if you want to go to the pictures!!!!

At the same time, I received a long letter from Auntie Rosa and some magazines have arrived today from her.

Mum, I wonder which photograph Mrs Dodgson would like because I will have one done for her if you like.

I had a very nice letter from Cousin Minnie and some snaps. She was telling me she was going to be cook at Christmas, they had a 14lb turkey.

Today I had a most odd letter from the BTH company, apparently they are sending them round to all employees asking what they want to do after the war. I am enclosing it, so let me know what you think of it and let me have it back please.

I did receive Auntie Ada's letter but so far have not replied. Don't bother her about the scarf because I have bought quite a nice one and it would be a pity to have it dyed, it would spoil it. (My pen has run out, please forgive pencil.) Is there enough of the wool (2 ply) to knit me a long-sleeved cardigan?

Don't bother about the pink cardigan. I am quite warm enough, Mum, I have an extra blanket now.

Do you remember I told you I was going to Kirkwall? Well, we went, and it rained the whole day, but we stayed the night and had quite a good time, eating three teas in all. It was nice to sleep in a different place, even if it was a Wrennery, the grub was good.

Coming back, we were on a small drifter and dash my buttons if a gale didn't blow up with the sea washing over so that we had to go down into the hold and one of the girls we were with was terribly sick. Actually, I was enjoying it in spite of the cold and, when it was calmer and drier, I went on deck and watched the ships and the mainland wreathed in mist and clouds.

Mum, if you go out at all, could you order those Cash's name tapes please?

Don't bother about apples, Mum, we get quite a few! The only thing I would like before I come home on leave (which is only seventy days now) is just a little something, either a tin of jam or a jellie or blancmange or something for our birthday party on the 15th of February, only don't bother about a cake, it'll be easier for you to send something in a tin.

Well, Mums, Dad and Joseph, that's all for now.

Tons of love,

Mary

12

Snow, Less and More

February 14th St Valentine's Day

I leave the car at Yesnaby and head south towards the stack of Yesnaby castle. It's a cold, bright, snow-sprinkled crispy underfoot day. No one around. I'm all alone, no other cars around, and I notice I'm following tracks of a lone mountain biker. They must be mad – cycling over these slippery, snowy rocks and frozen mud, often pretty close to the cliffs. At one point, they got off to push – on the uphill stretch past the sea stack, a set of footprints appeared, only to vanish again when they reached the level top. The tracks led across the headland on the narrow path, through short-cropped stunted wind-blasted heather. At first, I thought there were two bikes, but realised later that they marked the outward and return journey of a solitary cyclist. The wind is behind me, not strong, and I tread carefully. Where streams cross the path, the water gurgles under ledges of ice at the rims of stones. It's freezing, but the sun's out and I feel fine.

It's been a horrible week, adjusting to the shock of the February cold at 59°N after two months of 30°C at latitude 3.5°S. Horrible also to leave a loved one and go back to being alone, apparently for no good reason! Worse this time than last time when I first left, after I finished my job in Tanzania. Coming back to the UK after five years away, there were projects: a minor operation to sort out my cataract, and a major one, sorting out the old house in Stafford, ready for the move to Orkney. My parents' treasures – pottery, teapots, old cameras, thousands upon thousands of photographs, colour slides and prints, a tapestry from Egypt, an RAF tray, too heavy to be of any use, diaries, my grandmother's and great auntie's jewellery – such as it is, not very grand, but still there, still to be dealt with. Letters: my letters to my parents, my mother's letters to her parents, a lover's letters to me. Books. My son's toys: Lego, Thomas the Tank engine figures, cars, the set of Children's Encyclopaedias he won for writing a letter to the *Young Telegraph*. It was a letter about travelling by train, and how it was so much better than going by car. Ironic that he's now making promotional videos for an international car company. Too much furniture; too many tables, chairs, bookshelves, pictures. And I had friends to help with the decision making, to give me permission to either throw something out or keep it, to put in the charity shop pile, or the pile for the tip, or to sell. Friends to make a cup of tea and have a laugh with in between sorting. I had a goal: the move, and a new life, the excitement of discovery.

Now, though, I'm here – back to my new life. Sorted and settled, more or less, with new friends. After several months, it doesn't feel so new any more. In comparison with Africa, it feels small, predictable; what's worse is that, after two months of living with someone intimately, I'm alone again. My mind goes round in circles, always coming back to the stupidity of not talking properly sooner, avoiding discussion, living in the present. Not that I didn't try, but when a question is referred to as a can of worms, it has a tendency to put one off opening it, certainly at that time of night when one of us has to go to work and be on form the next day. I feel pathetic, a sixty-four-year-old adolescent, in love and as fragile as a teenager. I read emails and weep.

There are practical things still to do. A tooth chipped while eating fruit salad in Tanzania needed mending, so I found an NHS dentist. It's a brand-new surgery in Stromness, all gleaming white walls, deluxe lie-back dental couch, and shining state of the art equipment. I'm the second patient on the first day of opening. She does the usual check-up, mends the broken tooth and does an X-ray. On the way out, I'm astonished at how little I have to pay. Does that include the filling? Oh yes, comes the reply, that *is* for the filling. Check-ups are free in Scotland; another good reason to move to Orkney. It was so different and more painless than Mum's experience on her arrival on Hoy. The injections now are so specialised that the effect is quick acting and short-lived; gone are the days of going back into the waiting room until the thing took effect, or having to wait for hours (days, according to her!) until the numbness wore off.

★ ★ ★

A couple of days later, the wind has changed and the dustsheet on the washing line is swinging towards me; wind from the SE and rain lashing against the kitchen windows. I meet a friend in the Pomona, an establishment at the greasy spoon end of the coffee shop continuum. We have hot chocolate and talk about taxes and pensions and part-time jobs. Then I leave to trawl the charity shops for a suitable bag to take to London to visit my son. The rain and wind makes almost everyone walk with a hunched and pinched look. My body, soft and moist in Africa, becomes tense, dry and shrivelled.

The wind drops and I go to Marwick Bay. The waves are huge. Standing on the shore, I seem to be lower down than them – they must be twelve foot high. The surf is whipped up, glossy as royal icing. Tumbleweed globs of café au lait froth roll in a wind-blown dance over the rocks. Some of them are decorating the rusty remains of the boiler from the wrecked Monomoy, a cargo ship that ran aground in 1896.

Out beyond the reef, the ocean is steely, with no white horses, just the swell built up after a few days of north-easterlies. The grass, yellow-brown on the low cliffs, battered and swept flat by the storms of wind and waves, scorched by salt spray. Each step of my boots squeezes out water from the sodden substrate. Never mind maritime heath, I think, this is more like marine heath. The tide is out and, down on the beach, I look again for a *groatie buckie,* a cowrie shell *Cypraea europaea*. In the months of coming here, I've not yet found one. Today, amongst the yellow, pink, purple and maroon periwinkles, the pearly top shells and the pale whelks, there it is, my first groatie buckie, white and delicate, and I pick it up, striped on my black glove.

Further round on my circuit, outside the cow barn at Langskaill Farm, stands a sack of 'special minerals' from Birsay Farmers. The kye in unison lift their heads as they hear me passing, two rows of heads all turn simultaneously, stopping their munching. They probably think they might be getting some more special minerals from me.

I'm thinking about my mum. How she'd love to be here now. As I've been reading her letters, I've found her warmth and feeling for her parents so tangible, shining through the pages.

An only child born to an older mother, she was especially close to her family. She told the story of being taken to the doctor once as a young child and at the end of the consultation the doctor asked if there was anything else he could do for her (they said that even in those days!). She said yes, would he bring them a baby? She'd heard that doctors bring them in their black bags.

"Well," said the doctor with a sideways glance, "we'll have to see what the weather does, won't we, Mary?"

My grandmother, in her forties and deeply embarrassed by this, marched her home in angry silence – and Mum never did get a little brother or sister.

She was constantly writing letters to relatives and family friends, and she maintained many friendships throughout her life, as well as continually forging new ones through work and social activities. Here in Orkney, she was longing to see them again in Sheffield, counting the days to the next leave – ninety, seventy, fifty – and when eventually she went back, she was back to stay.

My grandmother in that year, 1945, was sixty-six – with new teeth, corsets and was frequently exhorted by my mother to 'rest'. What went wrong in my life, I wonder, that I'm sixty-four and starting again in a new place? It can't be all my fault – can it? At least I still have all my own teeth. And no corset.

I feel envious, and guilty, remembering how selfish I've been, and how many times I let her and my father down; how hurt they must have been by my wanderings, my unsuitable relationships, and lack of desire to come home. Even as a single mother when it would have been the obvious, easiest thing to go back and live with them – they had plenty of room – I wouldn't.

My mother left her sixty-four-year-old mother to go to Orkney, I left my sixty-two-year-old mother to go to Seychelles, and now my son is leaving his sixty-four-year-old mother to go to Dubai. Now I understand how Mum must have felt.

Always too independent, a rolling stone. I'd never understood that expression about gathering no moss. Surely it's a good thing not to gather moss? It only has to be dug out of gutters, scraped off paths, scratched out of lawns. Much later, I finally got it. My parents had their place, with the accumulated knowledge of years of living there. The neighbours all knew them, the friends went back for years. They were embedded in their community and settled like a stone in a mossy wall. Whereas me, I'm an exposed piece of newly fallen cliff. Yes, I have history, but only if you can read the story in the strata.

What makes me like this? An old boyfriend, an eternity

ago, regretting our separation, wondered in frustration: "How can you catch a swallow?"

Another friend, a wanderer too, also expressed it in terms of bird migration.

"It's like those arctic terns, they circle the globe, flying constantly, waiting to land, and they only land to breed. I'm still waiting to land."

Most birds have a reason to migrate. They move to find better food sources according to the season, or to breed in more favourable conditions. The ancient murrelet, however (what a name!), a bird related to puffins and guillemots, migrates huge distances for no apparent reason. Breeding in western Canada, they then fly across the northern Pacific to winter in Japan at a similar latitude and in a comparable environment. Pointless migration?

Could it be genetic? Recently I read[19] about the discovery of a gene D4DR that codes for a dopamine receptor. Dopamine is a neurotransmitter in the brain that is involved with reward. Basically, the more dopamine you have, the more you recognise reward and therefore sense of pleasure. However, if there is something wrong with the receptor, if it is damped down, then more and more 'rewards' are needed to achieve the same response. A variant of this gene, D4DR-7 repeat, has been shown to reduce the response to dopamine and those with the variant exhibit more novelty seeking behaviour; they are thrill-seekers.

Higher frequencies of the variant have been found in

---

19 *The Gene: an intimate history* by Siddhartha Mukherjee p.386 Scribner (May 2, 2017).

nomadic populations. What's more, with increasing distance from Africa, where migration of humans first began, the frequency of the gene variant increases, suggesting that the presence of the variant is a factor in the urge to migrate. In the home birds who stayed in Africa, the gene variant is rare; in those populations who left, it's more common. Perhaps that could explain my restlessness. Although, as often with genetics, it's not that simple: there could be ten or more genes involved, the D4DR variant accounts for a small proportion of thrill seeking, and then there's the effect of environment and culture. Still, if even some of it is in the genes, maybe I can feel less guilty about it.

I did write, of course, regularly from Seychelles, and tried to make up for it later, but really, was it too little and too late? They wouldn't have said that, forgiving as they were; the prodigal daughter returned and was treated far better than she deserved.

Mum was the home bird, not Dad. I wonder if he had the D4DR variant and passed it on to me. He would have travelled, I think, but events conspired against him. They were discussing emigration to Australia, the £10 assisted passages, when my grandfather, Mum's Dad, died, and they couldn't/ wouldn't leave my grandmother. Not long after that, he left his job as an accountant at a large bakery for some reason shrouded in mystery, and returned to the firm where he'd done his accountancy training. He stayed with that firm, taking it over as a partnership of two until not many years before he retired, when they in turn were taken over by much bigger fish; the world was changing, and he'd been left behind. Many years later, I found out that he'd uncovered dodgy practices of some kind at the baker's, but when he protested against these he was told to shut up or get out. Looking back, I realise this must have shocked him to the core. He was very ethical and balked against even the tiniest whiff of sharp practice or tax evasion, so he got out.

★ ★ ★

Rae is drinking coffee and we look out of the kitchen window at the mess of my back 'garden' or back field to be more accurate. It's a tangle of thistle stalks, still miraculously standing, and brown tussocky grass that the wind has done its best to scour and flatten. What's to be done with it?

"Horses," he says. "You could get a horse, or Shetland ponies mebbe. Kristen up the road might give ye the lend of a horse." I'm not keen on either horses or Shetland ponies, the latter having a reputation for bad-temperedness. "Or get yersel a loan of a couple of kye," he says. "Jimmy Walls'd mebbe give ye a loan." Goats, we'd already discussed, and he'd said the only Orcadian he knows who has anything to do with goats is Nanny Cheesegood, and "you don't want to go getting mixed up with her…" I didn't ask why not. Rae's established that most often, when you hear of goats in Orkney, they're kept by English – and we don't want to be too English, do we? "Sheep, now, you don't want to get sheep, 'cos they die."

???

"Oh yes," he says, "they say if ye buy a sheep, buy a good sharp spade…"

So, we're back to horses, and the next day I bump into him in the Post Office, Kristen's shop. "Oh aye," she says, "I can give ye a loan of my stallion, Eric." Rae and K talk electric fences. Her brother has one of hers that might already be on my field. "The good thing about a stallion is they always do their poo in the same place," she informs me, "very useful, so they're not messing all over the place." I say I'll call in to her house, Flanders, up the road a bit, to talk about it.

The hares are back in their spot at the back. I say hares, but today is the first day there are two. They blend in so well, blotchy light brown, and sit so still that at a quick glance you'll never see them; only if there's a flick of a dark ear, or a dark eye is open, will they be spotted.

For the last week, I've seen only one young one, in the same patch as last year, and wondered if that was where it had been born – but now, with a brighter, rusty patch on the back of its neck, is another. As the sun dips goldenly down to the western hills, they start lolloping about, poking at the grass, trying to find new growth: there's not much around yet.

Late February and the snowiest morning so far: it's easy to see the hares in this, as two of them charge across the field. You can see why it's a good idea for the Mountain Hares to turn white in the winter and get camouflaged. I put some old bread out for the birds, and the only taker at first is a hooded crow. Very tentatively, for a crow, it surveys the scene and stands on the gravel looking around. At last, it takes to the air with a little jump and lands very briefly on the stone, quite delicately (for a crow) grabbing a piece of crust and retreats to a safe distance to eat it. Then back it comes for more, but still doesn't settle, takes its chunk and leaves.

The wind is coming from the north-west, bitterly cold; snow lies in patches and rabbit-dug scrapes on the way up to Marwick Head. The clifftops are strangely becalmed. The fulmars are in full flight mode, soaring over navy-blue, white-tipped waves. Some of them are exceedingly plump and lunge out from the cliff into the up draught, weighed down by their belly, undercarriage dangling, wings slightly bent; they remind me of a crinolined lady holding out her skirts. At the top of their ascent they seem to stall, do a shivery shake of the wings and swoop back down again. It looks like they're really enjoying themselves. They aren't feeding. What are they doing? Practising? Scouting for nest sites? Or simply having fun?

On the horizon, the light and dark clouds marble the sky, snow showers are swept in one after the other off the North Atlantic. Westray, to the north, is clear as a lino cut and has its own sprinkling of snow.

Although it's cold, it's rarely cold enough to stop you walking. Not in Orkney. Too windy maybe, but the cold one can live with, whereas in Tanzania, the heat is often a limiting factor in the walking. It's often too hot to feel like going for a walk, quite apart from the vexed question of *where* to walk. It's childishly pleasing to discover this fact, that Orkney has a simple, obvious advantage, a huge one-up on Tanzania on the walking weather front.

Usually, I'm the only one walking this circuit, but today I meet a couple and their dogs. She's short and stocky and he's tall and thin. Their dogs look like them.

It snows on and off all day, in between the sunny spells. Flurries of big flakes move swiftly across the island, reducing visibility, almost hiding the neighbours' houses. After one of them there's a snowbow on the hill behind; I gaze out of the kitchen window. The melted snow drips down from where the gutter droops and a screw has come out of the wall. Another thing to be fixed.

Pink clouds, white snow, black cattle, the only ones left out all winter. Thick pink low snow-filled clouds, and to the west, goose-grey with a peachy lining. The skies here are an entertainment in themselves.

Another major entertainment in the Orkney calendar at this time of the year is the Festival of One-Act Plays organised by the Scottish Community Drama Association. Every district seems to have its own drama club or two and the competition takes place over the course of a week, three plays being performed each night.

"Are you going every night?" Margaret asks me. I'm quite taken aback by this, having decided to go only on the two nights when the Birsay Drama group – my local team – are on. "Only, we usually go to all of them," she adds. I stick with my two nights.

It's a girls' night for our little Birsay crowd, packed into Margaret's car. The auditorium of the Orkney Theatre is packed, and the plays are great. There are comedies like: a farcical pantomime within a play, a classic, "The Steamie" set in a Glaswegian wash-house and the poignant "Flying with Swans" about three women friends and old age. After the plays, every evening, an adjudicator from 'Sooth' gives a critique of each performance and, at the end of the week, pronounces the verdict. The winning drama group will go to the national finals in Scotland later in the year. Great fun. Next year I'll be going every night.

So, I quickly regained my equilibrium and got over my lovesickness. What a pity it took me so long to understand that it's better to fall in love with the ones who love me rather than those who I *want* to love me! There's a summer ahead in which to reinforce old friendships and nurture new ones. How could I stay miserable for long?

Wren Tel L.M.Walker 94167
Haybrake
Lyness
Orkney
11ᵗʰ Jan 1945

My dear Mum and Dad and Uncle Bill,

I received your very very nice parcel today. You are so thoughtful, Mum, to put all those little things in I wanted. Uncle Bill, thanks for the money, it's very good of you, it certainly couldn't have come at a better time, fortunately. It's payday tomorrow and I only had about 1/- left. The almonds were lovely. Thanks also for your nice letter, Uncle Bill, which arrived at the same time as the parcel.

Sorry you spent New Year alone, I hope you are heaps better by now.

As usual, there is nothing new, really. We had a very good dance last night, which I thoroughly enjoyed, had a smashing time. You see, we have a sort of summer and winter sports club up at the signal station and we held it in the Wrennery and it was really good, a decent crowd and all the staff officers, etc., were in a very good mood. We had, unfortunately, to go on the morning watch and were terribly tired, but we slept all the next day till about 3.30pm.

We have seen the Northern Lights (Aurora Borealis) again recently when we came down from work at 2am. They were really lovely lighting up the northern sky with a pale green light with pinpoint rays like tiny searchlights of mauve and green darting hither and thither and then slowly fading. It was marvellous.

Just now (when the sun is shining) the hills are still covered with snow, and they look very lovely.

It is now Friday, and I have been working very hard indeed, with more concentration than I've _ever_ used in my long life.

Tonight we are going Scottish dancing.

Must go to supper now.

Heaps of love to all.

Hope you are all _very_ well and happy,

Mary Lilian

Wren Tel L.M.Walker 94167
WRNS Quarters
Haybrake
Lyness
Orkney
21/1/45

My dear Mum and all of you,

I received Uncle Bill's letter and your note today, very many thanks, it was a pleasant surprise also to receive the stamps, which were very welcome.

(Please forgive the pencil but I am writing on watch and it's easier than ink.)

Since I wrote to you last we have had a terrific amount of snow. Never have I in my wildest dreams imagined anything like it. The blizzards were terrific, and we had to walk up the hill to work and back because the buses could not get through, the drifts were so deep. It has been fearfully hard work ploughing one's way through against a biting headwind, but it was very exhilarating. It is really impossible to describe quite what it has been like – we have all had to cling together for fear anyone would get lost as the drifts have been more than waist deep. The blizzards have been unbelievably fierce, and we have been compelled to wear goggles when going to and from work, together with a couple of scarves, bells and two or three pairs of stockings. However, I have quite enjoyed it; as you know, I have always been fond of snow, but you have never seen the like of this lot we have had. It has had its compensations providing a good deal of fun in the way of snow fights with whatever members of the navy, army or marines have come across our path. The snow made the landscape even more lovely than usual and Betty and I together with two more girls were out for a

121

really superb walk one day. I don't think I have ever been for such a marvellous walk. It was the same way as we usually go, round the shore and back by the road, but no one had walked that way since the snow and it was about eighteen inches deep, with drifts in many places. It was a wonderful picture; the old wall, the bridge, the semi-frozen burn and the background of the hills and sea made the most perfect Christmas card scene imaginable. The sea was the weirdest shade of deep greeny brown. When we had been walking for about an hour and a half, we came across an old, deserted hut with a figure of Hitler in the window. We immediately set about firing snowballs at it, but were very unfortunate in our aims. Just then, a young blizzard sprang up and we turned for home, our cheeks stinging and glowing. We had only got a little way when some soldiers from a small unit nearby hailed us, and we were given a very welcome mug of hot tea and bread and butter. Such was the episode of our first day of snow. The next day, when we came off at 2am, we had hot soup and toast, which was very welcome after our hectic journey down.

Well, that's really enough of me in the snow, but it has so become part of our lives this last week that it is difficult to think of anything else to say.

So, I'll end on this chilly note and say – only sixty-four days!!

Heaps of love,

Mary

13

News

Wren Tel L.M.Walker
Haybrake
Lyness
19/1/45

My dear Mum and Dad and Joe,

I was very glad to have such a nice letter from you, Dad, last night, it was really grand to hear of all your doings. I was most surprised to hear you had been out in the blackout – I don't think I would overdo it if I were you, it's bad enough when you <u>have</u> to go, don't take too many risks. However, I am so glad you have both been out. Every letter I have from everyone who knows us tells me how wonderfully well and years younger you look, don't you think it is better than winning all your blinking old pools?

I have had magazines from Auntie Rose and a letter, also a letter from Phyllis and Brenda, please thank them, I will try and write tomorrow.

I was horrified to hear of the murder in Ecclesall Road, it was a foul one and no mistake I hope they get the culprit.[20]

---

20   They never did find the culprit. It was indeed a horrible murder of one Eleanor Hammerton, a spinsterly, somewhat reclusive, but 'always friendly' shopkeeper whose age was given variously as seventy-five, seventy-nine and eighty. She was battered to death

It's very good of you to bother about the cake, Mum, thanks a lot.

Have done nowt since you heard from me last except sleep – oh, I played a table tennis match with some fellows from a nearby camp and lost, needless to say.

Mum, Pat is getting married on her next leave, so Flo is going down about Friday to stay till early Sunday morning and, as she has invited us all, I have asked Betty to stay a couple of nights with us, that'll be okay, won't it, Mum?

Now I am going to pack up as I have few more notes to write.

Heaps of love,

Mary xxxx

> *Wren Tel L.M.Walker*
> *Haybrake*
> *Lyness*
> *4th Feb 45*
> *0530 hrs*

My dear Mum and Dad and Pieface,

At this unearthly hour, you'll be tucked up in your nice warm beds for another few hours – heavenly!!! I received your lovely letters last evening, they had only taken twenty-four hours to come, which is very good.

I was so pleased to get the money, Dad, thanks a lot. I will put it in the bank straightaway or I'll be spending it, though what on I don't know. Dad, I nearly died laughing when I read about you finding the

---

in her draper's shop and found on Saturday, the 13th of January. She was said to sleep on a couch in the back room downstairs and 'in recent years had never undressed'. http://www.chrishobbs.com/sheffield4/eleanorhammerton1945.htm

ten-bob note. I can just imagine you laughing, Mum, when Dad told you about it, it's the funniest thing I've heard in ages – you must tell Mr Beaumont when you see him. Dad, your cheerfulness shows in your letters, which are really smashing.

Glad the snow has gone, it has gone here too; for how long, I don't know.

It was grand to hear about the Playhouse opening again, really the best news I've heard for ages. Many thanks for the book of crossword puzzles, I have been doing some tonight. With regard to the draught board, I regret to inform you that I have lost it, I cannot think where it is, unless it is at Thurso. The girls were doing it that Sunday night when we were stranded there and I did it once and I think that I must have left it, we were in such a rush; we had to be up so early, I must have left it lying around. Can you get another? It would be very useful if you could.

About the 'eats'…

Could you send:

1. _Tin jam_ – strawberry or raspberry or something _original_ preferred.
2. Tin _Spam._
3. Tin peanut butter.

Very urgent.

That's all, no cake or anything. Thanks a million!!

Sorry to hear of Auntie Roza's misfortune, she really is unlucky. Dad, remember me to Mr Stainrod when you go to see the old boy. We must go to the Playhouse both weeks when I am home. Yes, the war certainly seems to be going well at the moment, I hope it will continue thus.

That's all now.
Love, lots of it,
from
Mary
PS It is exactly one year yesterday since I received my calling up papers – does it seem longer? Mum – I do hope your hands are less painful – take care of yourself, old bean!!!!!!
Love. LM

Wren Tel L.M.Walker
WRNS Quarters
Lyness
Orkney
6th Feb

Dearest Mums and all,

How the time is simply flying – only fifty more days now before I am home. So glad to hear you have finished the film – I hope you will be able to get another because I have little chance of doing so up in Kirkwall, so do try, dears.

Tonight, I have had four letters, one from my old faithful friend Dorothy, one from Rachel and one from Phyllis, and a sweet letter from Brenda in which she tells me she is looking after you all.

When I read how all my friends are faring, I am inclined to be glad I am here in my present state. I am sure I am much happier than many, both physically and mentally, and particularly emotionally. Dorothy, while still in love with her Tim, is inclined to think about the fun we used to have together, she likes so many of the same things as me, I do hope she will be <u>sure</u> when the time comes, it would be awful if she took the fatal plunge and then found out too late. Rachel fortunately <u>has</u>

found out apparently and has broken off her romance with that horrid man whose photograph I hated so much. Betty Foster (now Miller), Rachel tells me, is having a baby in July, which will keep her quiet, ha ha!

David Franklin has been home from Holland on leave and is very well. Frank Marsden had to have one eye out to save the sight of the other and now has a glass one, poor lad. I wonder if he still retains his remarkable sense of humour!!

So much for my friends and their news – oh no! Just one more item. Do you remember Sylvia Stirrup's sister, the one who married the hairdresser at Atkinson's, now in the RAF? She has lost her husband.

Many thanks for the papers, it is good to see a bit of Sheffield. I was sorry to read of the death of Mr Wackerbarth, a very good friend to the YWCA – a nice chap. Mr Nunweek I see has popped off too, poor old lad. Miss Hensman will miss him. Did I ever tell you the old b... (Miss H) sent me a hanky at Christmas, which had been used obviously and which I cut up for dress shields in my new green frock? I have not written to her because I have written two <u>long</u> letters to her, and she has never troubled to write to me. I <u>won't</u> go back to work for her if I have to beg from door to door – I'd rather starve.

You will be pleased to know I am starting cooking classes – the leatherwork is not going so well. Betty and I have been so lazy lately, by the time we get up, the classes are closed and Uncle Bill, dear, I was trying to make you a purse, but I'm afraid, old duck, it won't be finished for your birthday, but I will hurry up and make an effort this week. I seem to be so busy, never a moment to spare.

I was at church again on Sunday night – a new minister, a pleasant, cheery man who looks like Uncle Jack has arrived. We now have tea and biscuits, which gives the service an added attraction. Do you remember me telling you about that sweet little beard I met at a dance last week? He was at church and was singing afterwards, a lovely voice, and a face like the pictures of the old prophets and apostles. Just listen to me – soppy thing.

This drivel must cease, or you will think I am 'nuts'. By the time you wade through this scrawl, Dad, it will be dinner time and I will have kept you so long that you will be finding at least a couple of £1 notes.

Heaps of love, Mary

PS This scrawl is terrible, please forgive.

> *Wren Tel L.M.Walker*
> *Haybrake*
> *RN Base*
> *Lyness*
> *9.2.45*

My dear Mum and all,

I was so very pleased and thrilled to receive your lovely letters yesterday. Mum, how can you talk about expecting me to be bored when they are always so lovely and interesting and full of news?

What a lot of nasty things have happened!! I was shocked to read about the woman at Auntie Ada's little shop. Very sorry to hear about Auntie Florrie, she would get a nasty shock, but maybe it will show her how silly she has been to keep money in the house. It is similar to the episodes that took place at the time Fred Rowbotham had their house ransacked.

I'm so sorry to hear about Hilary, I know Gladys will be very very troubled. Is it something to do with her nerves, do you think? I would not be inclined to let it rest at that, that she <u>might</u> be normal, I would go to other specialists until I got to the root of the matter.

Uncle Bill, thanks so much for your letter and for the 10/-, honestly you shouldn't have sent it, but I will put it in the bank out of harm's way because I'll probably need it when I go to Kirkwall again, thanks a lot!!

I can't imagine why you received a letter from me with an Edinburgh postmark but I'm glad you received it quickly at any rate.

When I come home, we'll have a quiet time with no big gatherings and we'll go out to different houses instead of such crowds coming to our house, except of course for Auntie Ada and Auntie Rose.

How is your nose? You must take care of it…

Uncle Bill, I do hope you have a nice birthday. I'm sorry I have no card, but I don't think you'll mind that. When I went to Kirkwall about three weeks ago, it was impossible to buy any. I still haven't finished your little purse, do forgive me, the spirit's very willing, but the flesh – ah me!!! – so weak, but it will arrive eventually.

We were over to the garrison cinema to see the film "Henry V" and thoroughly enjoyed it. I never enjoy a film <u>quite</u> as much as I would at home because of all the cracks made by the audience and Henry V was no exception to the rule, but half the island was there, so I expect it was only the usual thing.

Did I tell you that I was starting cookery classes? I of course do not need to learn cooking being very proficient at that art, ahem!!! Ahem!!!!!! But the idea is that we shall be able to buy the things we make, which will supplement our somewhat monotonous diet.

Last night, we began Norwegian classes for the first time, and I think I am going to like it. It is a similar language to our own in many respects with a lot of words common to both, and I quite enjoyed the first lesson. A Norwegian commander is taking the classes. So, you see, we don't have very much spare time these days, we never seem to have any time to laze around and, of course, there is washing and ironing to be done and stockings to be mended!!

I don't know whether I have told you, we were having a table tennis tournament – well, I was drawn to play with the wife of one of the officers from the office (actually, he is our Warrant Tel). She has only been up here a little while and they have a tiny bungalow a little way from the base (there are a few civilians living here). They have a little boy, John, who is seven and the image of his father. She came down to the rec and brought John and we had a very good game, though she absolutely wiped the deck up with me. She was really smashing.

Afterwards, I fetched in some tea and Ryvita and syrup and they stayed for about an hour and a half and we had quite a pleasant time. She had to do some shopping and went up to the civilian shopping centre (where we are not allowed to go) and brought me back some delicious cakes and tarts and shortbread – unfortunately, they did not go very far as eight of us shared them, but they were very good indeed.

I hope, Mum, by now you have received my letter asking for jam and Spam, not marmalade, as we have a 2lb tin of marmalade not opened yet. Betty does not like it anyway, okay?

By the way, you ask when I shall arrive home: Wednesday the 28th of March, I hope.

That's all for now.

Lots of love,

Mary

PS This business of Dad looking younger is getting serious. By the time I come home he will be minus one!

★ ★ ★

Mum sounds really chirpy in these letters and it's lovely to read that she's feeling so well in all respects. She has great support from close friends and plenty of dance partners! There's certainly lots to do and, in that respect, Orkney is still the same – like her, I don't know where the time goes! Before I moved, people used to ask what on earth I'd do during these long, dark, winter evenings, but as it turns out, I've done hardly any knitting and it's a treat to have an evening at home.

It's so frustrating to only get half the story in these letters! What did the woman do in Auntie Ada's little shop? What happened to Auntie Florrie – presumably she was burgled – and what about poor Hilary? Imagine some doctor telling her she *might* be normal! I'd love to know the answers to these puzzles – was it her nerves? Was there a spate of break-ins, maybe under cover of the blackout? So much for everyone pulling together for the war effort, which is what we usually hear about. Plus, it's only a couple of weeks since that horrible murder on Ecclesall Road.

"Having one eye out to save the sight of the other" puzzled me – how does this work then? I consulted my neurologist friend who explained it as "sympathetic ophthalmia", in which severe damage to one eye causes blindness in the other eye. Recognised by Hippocrates[21] in the first century BC, medical papers describe it as:

"A rare and blinding ocular complication due to ocular injury."

---

21   https://www.ncbi.nlm.nih.gov/pmc/articles/PMC3277011/

Although rare, it was the cause of blindness in Louis Braille. The development of the condition can be prevented by enucleation – removal of the whole eyeball. Once it starts, it's too late; removal of the damaged eye doesn't help. Even now the mechanism is unclear, but is thought to be due to some sort of autoimmune response. The idea is that trauma to one eye sets up an immune response in both eyes, which goes wrong and attacks the tissues of the eye itself. Treatment now is less radical than removal of the other eye and depends on the use of anti-inflammatory and immunosuppressant drugs. Poor Frank Marsden; even in wartime, the incidence of sympathetic ophthalmia was very rare, but presumably one eye was so damaged that they took it out as a pre-emptive strike.

The Norwegian connection is still strong in Orkney. Since Viking times, Orkney belonged to Norway, but Norway belonged to Denmark and King Christian I. It's a complicated tale of debt and dowry, property and pawn. In trying to disentangle the threads,[22] I came across the interesting and esoteric terms *impignoration* and *excambion*. Basically, the story as I understand it goes like this: Scotland owed a lot of money to Denmark for the rent of the Hebrides – 200 years' worth. Charles VII of France proposed a marriage between King Christian's daughter Margaret and James III-to-be of Scotland. This marriage contract, agreed in 1468, would cancel the annual rent and clear all the arrears, which seems like a very good deal for Scotland. Not only that, but as dowry, Denmark was supposed to pay 60,000 Rhine florins to

22   Charles Tait, *The Orkney Guide Book*.

Scotland!! (If only they could negotiate such an advantageous settlement in the Brexit/UK discussions!)

Very hard on Denmark – why on earth did they agree? Because they couldn't pay it: they could only afford 10,000, so Orkney was held in hock (impignorated) and Shetland was pawned the following year.

And what of 'excambion'? That simply means, in Scots law, the exchange of land, but as usual, nothing is simple. James III exchanged some land in Fife for Kirkwall Castle, then belonging to Earl Sinclair, but Earl Sinclair held on to a lot of the land in Orkney. Feuding continued, to put it mildly, and Orkney was ruled by a series of harsh and ruthless Earls until the 17th century.

As for the debt, that was never paid. Scotland insists that the right of Denmark to redeem Orkney and Shetland has passed into obscurity because of the history of rule from Edinburgh. Could this be a loophole, I wonder, to allow Orkney to revert to Danish rule and continue to be part of the EU?

Despite all the strife, complications and history of occupation, there's still an Orkney-Norway friendship association, but not an equivalent Danish one. There's a Nordic Studies centre, a huge woven wall-hanging in St Magnus Cathedral to signify the friendship, and they have big celebrations in Kirkwall on Norwegian Constitution Day, on the 17th of May.

"Will you come and carry a flag on the 17th?" someone asks. Unfortunately, I'm going to be away that day, so can't participate in Norway-Orkney relations.

"Why are we so friendly with Norway?" I wonder, but there's no real answer; something to do with the populations of Norway being decimated by the Black Death? Perhaps the link was strengthened during World War II? Maybe it's the camaraderie of two nations previously ruled by Denmark? Whatever the reason, unlike in 1944, they no longer have Norwegian language classes!

Wren Tel L.M.Walker
Haybrake
RN Base
Lyness
ORKNEY
14th Feb

My dear Mum and all,

Very many thanks for the parcel received today. The lemon curd is very good, we look like having a real feast tomorrow night. Betty has had two huge parcels containing sweets, oranges, apples, nuts and oatcakes (tons of 'em) and cheeses and jam and syrup. Flo has had cakes and Pat has got a parcel too, so we shan't starve.

After we have eaten, we are going on to a dance, but I doubt whether we'll get that far, we'll be quite ill. It is rather a pity we had decided to have our party tomorrow because Betty and I had another invitation, but we had arranged it because it is the only evening we are all off together and we are going to have a real beano. Betty and I have been playing a lot of table tennis lately and we were playing on Tuesday in a tournament and one of the officers asked us if we would play in a match against a team of officers from a certain ship. However, we had to refuse very reluctantly and forgo the prospect of a very pleasant evening because we could not let the others down. However, the officer said that other dates would be fixed up with various ships and we would definitely be on the team. (Incidentally, the tournament is to be continued next week, I happen to be leading and mean to win if at all possible.)

The Norwegian lessons are going fine, and I quite like the language.

Mum, dear, I have written to Auntie Florrie as you asked me and have sent a large box of oranges to Auntie Roza. I do hope it's not a case of "sending coals to Newcastle" and I hope they are not bad on arrival. We have had a lot of the same lately and I have eaten as many as five in a day – don't faint, Mum – I have eaten at least eighteen this week!!!!!!

You should see us going to the cinema eating oranges. You see, going to the cinema here is a sort of duty, almost, and is a biweekly date. All our watch – eight girls – are all on very good terms, we are all good pals and we meet in the canteen and have tea together, and then proceed to the cinema armed with a large box of oranges (skinned) and pockets full of "nutty" (naval for sweets). We all sit together, usually behind some of the "sparkers" from the office and aim pips under cover of darkness – very unladylike, but good fun, and we <u>are</u> <u>all</u> ladies. Today we went to see "A Canterbury Tale", which I enjoyed very much.

Uncle Bill, I hope you have had a pleasant time on your birthday. I drink to your health now, you old dogsbody – in a cup of strong cocoa; I cannot help wishing it were champagne or even cider.

Heaps of love,
  Mary
  Xxx

Wren Tel Walker LM
Haybrake
Lyness
16ᵗʰ Feb

My dear Mum and all,

Many thanks for your nice letter received at midnight last night, it was a lovely surprise. The photographs seem pretty good, what do you think? I would like some more prints please. Six of the big group and six of <u>one</u> of the ones with Mr Toft on, thanks very much.

Pancakes, you said!! We never even smelt a pancake, but I'm hoping to smell quite a few in six weeks' time. (Less than six now, my! How quickly time flies these days.)

Just imagine you having snow on Sunday; here it was like spring and beautifully sunny. We went out without our greatcoats on but then we have been having better weather than you all the time.

I had a nice long letter from Margaret Shaw yesterday.

I will continue this tomorrow, I have nothing else to say today – oh yes – we had the eats yesterday and they were very good. Pat and Flo went to Kirkwall and brought some bread back, nice white new bread, and we had a pound of fresh butter given to Flo by a kind friend, so it was very good. Betty Williamson had a tin of pineapple which she opened. We went to a dance afterwards, but it was not very bright, so we came back early. Tonight, we are "gold-braiding", going to a "middies" dance, so the eats should be good, if nothing else.

17ᵗʰ Feb

Less than forty days now and I will be home, it seems no time at all since I said it would be ninety-nine days!!!!

Well, I went to the midshipman's dance last night, middies and junior officers of the flagship, and I had a lovely evening. A good many of the fellows were very much like John Powell, the same type of boy, but there were quite a few who were older, and I spent a pleasant evening in the company of a 6'5" warrant officer. The eats were good too and it wasn't the "beery" affair that many of these "dos" are.

Mother, my old duck, I have another request to make, once more; you will be tired of sending parcels off to me. Will you send off to me <u>by return please</u> my little navy-blue coat? You see, I have my skirt, but do not always want to wear my raincoat when going out in civvies. Please register it!!! Thanks so much, Mum.

The marmalade is lovely, Mum – we are still eating our anniversary things, we had so many. Thanks so much for sending those things off to Mrs Burnett, she has been sending really super parcels lately.

How is the cutlery situation now? Do you think it would be possible to get any more by the time I come on leave? Will you let me know?

That's all for now, so cheerio and tons of love.
Mary

PS It was not a <u>matelot</u> with a beard, Mum, but a Lieut. Okay????

Wren Tel L.M.Walker
Haybrake
Lyness
20th Feb
0400

My dear Mum and all,
I received your lovely parcel yesterday afternoon – thanks so much.

Betty also thanks you for the jam and her mother has written to say how pleased they are with the things you sent them. The pullover is absolutely smashing and fits me perfectly, do thank Clara for me. I have another 6oz of wool here from Comforts, which will no doubt come in handy sometime.

I am sorry, dears, to keep causing you so much trouble regarding parcels, I hope you have sent off my little coat – I can assure you it will <u>definitely</u> be the last thing before I go on leave, but it is a necessary article <u>really</u>. You see, we have had some lovely days, particularly at the weekends, and last weekend I was out in civvies but unfortunately had to wear my scruffy old raincoat, which wasn't so good. It's rather nice to wear civvies for walking because then we needn't wear hats and it's rather good walking out on Sunday afternoons in this spring-like weather we have been having.

I have had a letter from Arthur again; he is very chocker now and is hoping for a spot of shore leave – he has not had any for eighteen months, so is naturally not feeling too good.

Do thank Brenda for the peanut butter. I have so many tins in my drawer it looks like a grocery store – I shall have heaps of odds and ends to send home, I have accumulated so much stuff, but it is such a bother going down to the BMO to have every fiddling little parcel censored. I don't think I'll bother about the collars, Mum. I'll do them myself for the time being.

I have no news at all. I have done nothing since I wrote you last except go walking and canteening. Yesterday, we were at Norwegian, but we have a new teacher, Lieut RNVR, a "sweet little boy" who is an intelligence officer here. Unfortunately, the other man, the Norwegian commander, had to go, but the new man is very good. We have a very busy week in front of us. Betty and I are doing such

*a lot this week, but I will write later and tell you what we have been
doing.*

Hope you are keeping okay, Mum.
Tons of love,
Lilian Mary

> *Wren Tel L.M.Walker*
> *Haybrake*
> *Lyness*
> *21/2/44*

My dear Mums and all,

*How quickly the time is flying by. I had a letter from Auntie Roza,
so glad she has received the oranges safely, I thought she would like
them. She told me you had been to see her and that you still had a lot
of neuritis. I do hope you're feeling a little better, Mum.*

*I must tell you about our day off this week. As usual, we stayed
in bed until after lunchtime. We had planned to go to leatherwork
but, as usual, we dilly-dallied until it was very late and it was such
a wonderful day, we decided to go for a walk instead. We didn't start
out till 4.15pm and began to walk the opposite way to the road we
usually go. It was really a glorious day and wonderfully sunny, the
sea was a really vivid blue and everything was very peaceful. Spring
seemed to be very near at hand. We walked down past all the little huts
and conglomeration of odd little buildings that make up the base. Just
as we were by the laundry, a lorry stopped and the man asked if we
wanted a lift later on, when he'd finished at the laundry. Of course,
we said yes, and we walked on until we came to a tiny little old chapel
with an ancient humpy graveyard. We went to explore and found some
interesting things about the folk who were buried there. The little place*

was looking out on to the sea, and we thought what a peaceful resting place for those folk who have spent all their lives by the sea. The road by the sea was rather like Derwent or Bradfield, the islands are so near, it was more like being by a huge lake. Nearby, a ploughing match was going on, and the gulls were whirling and screaming overhead. Against the vivid blue sky and the sea it made a marvellous picture.

Just then, the lorry stopped, and we got in the front. Apparently, the two men in the back were from a little trawler and they were looking for a house where they could buy some spuds. It was funny because they had lost the address, so we had to stop at every two-storeyed house we came to. However, there aren't many of them, so we were okay. We skimmed along past all the tiny, thatched crofts on the shore until we came to the Admiral's house. We went up the side road and eventually found the place we wanted, which was a prosperous looking farm almost on the top of the cliffs. The view from the top was superb to say the least of it. We could see the north coast of Scotland quite plainly and it was grand. The cliffs are very high and rocky just there and reminded me of Cornwall. While the men were getting the 'tatties', the lorry driver took us to see a tiny chapel in the grounds of the Admiral's house (of course, I don't suppose we should have officially been there). It was a lovely little place, which smelt so fusty and ancient that we thought it hadn't been used for centuries. In the wall was a stone cross, which the inscription said had been found near the spot and was about the time 900AD. Not bad, eh!!

By this time, it was nearly 5.30 and there wasn't time to walk back, so we came all the way in the lorry and it was a very pleasant trip.

Now I'll leave this and write more tomorrow – we are just going to the Music Circle and I'll give you the programme tomorrow.

Thursday 22nd

It was pleasant to listen to good music. The programme included Rossini, Thieving Magpie, Mozart's Magic Flute, Strauss Artist's Life, Handel selections from Messiah, and some Gilbert and Sullivan, so you see it was very varied.

You will laugh when I tell you about this. Do you remember I told you I had been playing the wife of our officer at table tennis? Well, they have asked me to tea next week. Betty knows, of course, but I haven't mentioned it to <u>anyone</u> else – there would be quite a lot of remarks and 'green eyes' if some of the others knew I was so well-in. Don't you think it's funny?

You will be pleased to know our next leave list is out and I go together with Pat, Flo and Betty on a smashing date – the 27th of July – so I shall, all being well, be home for Bank Holiday week, so I know Dad you'll be pleased – what do you think about that????

I think that's all for now.

Tons of love,

Mary

Xxxxx

PS This is being written under difficulties, so please forgive the writing.

14

Being Poorly

At the beginning of March, we have a couple of bright, calm days, but I'm inside feeling miserable with a raging sore throat and temperature. I feel sorry for myself. This is when you want someone to chat and take your mind off it, or at the very least, make you a cup of tea.

It's the season for ploughing matches.

The fields already ploughed are the only ones which still have snow on them – they must stay colder, you'd think being brown they'd be warmer – and across the road the Arty farmer is ploughing, followed by a snow-dome chaos of gulls. Yesterday he was muck-spreading; a fresh countryside aroma fills the air, and the neighbours make sure no washing is hanging out to catch the scent. A wren darts around the shrubs in the front garden, apparently enjoying the unaccustomed lack of wind.

A few days later, I'm still inside. Friends come, bearing throat sweets, paracetamol and books. I'd casually let them know about my poorliness, having woken up one morning and not had any contact for a few days (well, maybe only two) and thought – who would know if I died? This living alone is for young people, those who go out to work, not for old people or those who stay at home.

A ring-tail hen harrier whizzes by outside the front window. A thousand starlings are competing on my wall for a batch of failed ginger biscuits, made when I was in bad shape on Saturday and not even worth keeping for emergencies. Remember in future: only do baking when on good form.

Wren Tel L.M.Walker
Haybrake
Lyness
4/3/45

My dear Mum and all,

Do please forgive the blunt pencil but I don't seem to have my knife with me just now. I expect you will be wondering how I am faring!

Well, it is only two days since I came in sick bay, but they are the longest two I have spent since I joined the Wrens. However, my throat is heaps better and, if I don't come out soon, I shall die of boredom. I am cooped up in a small room on my own and I am the only one in the whole sick bay. I have an army of nurses to wait on me, but I hate being in bed, especially as, apart from my throat being very bad, I have never really felt ill of myself. To lie here seeing the sun streaming in and thinking of Betty and co out to tea on a destroyer makes me mad – but enough of this mood. I received your nice cheerful letter, Dad, this morning. At the same time came lots of other letters, all to cheer me up. You see, they won't let the girls visit me yet, so they all wrote me funny little letters, which really did cheer me up immensely. I had one from Betty, of course, giving me a long account of the day's doings, one from Pat, one from Alma, the girl who sleeps in the next bed to me and is a born comedian, and one from Ian, a very nice fellow in the office, and one from his pal also in the office, a leading Tel – they are a funny pair. I must save all the letters to show you as my war souvenirs!!!

I forgot to tell you in my haste to write to you on Friday that I had received the parcel. Thanks awfully, Mum – I should have worn the coat this weekend, was I mad?!!! The mittens and scarf are fine, I will try and write to Mrs Dodgson tomorrow. Sorry about Brenda, hope she is better, also Miss Kirkham.

We saw crocuses outside a cottage here the other day, so it makes me feel that spring is here, though the winds here are still very treacherous.

So glad to hear about you sending the papers, it will help pass the day tomorrow. I expect I'll be here another few days yet. I should very much like to see Mrs Dodgson's book about the Orkneys, do save it till I come home. The soldier you speak of must be at Stromness, Dad, which is on the main island where Kirkwall is. We are planning to go there next week.

Three weeks tomorrow I'll be home, it seems unbelievable, and no time at all since I came back from leave.

It is now 8.30pm and I have had my supper and late cup of tea and will soon be settling down for the night. This is a tiny room with cream and green walls and green iron bedstead and polished hospital floors. It's strange having the whole run of the place, but I can't help wishing there was someone else here.

Mrs "Captain" was in yesterday and First Officer and I'm hoping the gang will be able to come tomorrow.

Apparently, I missed some fun in the cabin the other night, a small rat (or was it a large mouse) was caught. We have been troubled for some time with these beasts, which have been getting into drawers and eating people's jumpers, etc., etc., so the rat man came at last and laid *down sticky paper. The girls were awakened by squeaks and Flo hit the intruder with her shoe, but I hope they have got rid of them. They are a blinking menace and attacked my 'nutty' one night.*

You will be pleased to know I am having smashing eats in here and even I find difficulty in wading through the mountains of dinner. I managed a first course today of terrific chunks of beef and veg but stuck at the eleventh prune when it came to the sweet course.

Well, my little cherub-pie, I think I'll have to stop now, I'm getting sleepy.

Tons of love,
Mary

PS Do thank Auntie Roza for the syrup, I hope she is much better, will write soon.

PPS We are all getting LEAVE together! (This is the umpteenth time I have told you this, folks.)

Wren Tel L.M.Walker
Haybrake
Lyness
ORKNEY
6th March

My dear Mum and all,

Tuesday and I am still here alone in splendid isolation and in a pretty green and cream ward quite empty with only the sound of the seagulls and the ever-persistent moaning of the wind for company. However, I am quite better now and there is only one tiny minute spot of yellow on my throat and the doctor says I will be out either tomorrow or Thursday morning.

At the moment, there is a fire in the corner of the ward, and I am sitting by it. There is a bookcase full of good books, which I have been sampling, and it is altogether a too luxurious and comfortable state of existence for me, especially the delicious eats we have here. I feel like a pretender; if I had felt ill, it would have been a different matter, but I'm perfectly well.

I have not been able to see any of my friends, which has been a nuisance, but I have had innumerable letters from them and also oranges, chocolates and magazines.

Today I sneaked a look at my medical record sheet (here there are details of my medical at Bramall Lane – do you remember what a state I was in? Strangely enough, it is an excellent report, everything being good – and against "mental and nervous character" it said "Alert and stable" – very funny!!!!!).

I do hope it's fine on Thursday – we have planned to go over to Rackwick, round by the coast road for about fourteen miles (we are going in a small van with a fellow we met a little while ago who goes every week) and are hoping to walk back through the hills, so I do hope it's a nice day.

That's all for now. Three weeks today I will be on the boat now on my way home – it seems unbelievable, the time passes so quickly.

So long. Hope you are all very well.

Love (lots of it) Mary

PS I dreamt last night that Uncle Bill backed his car into a wheelbarrow full of soil; it happened in Pitsmoor Rd. The first night I was in here I had the most vivid dream I have ever had in my life – I dreamt I was suddenly transported into your bed, Mum, and I could see your little "cupid clock" and I heard the telephone ring so plainly and you and

Dad and Beryl Taylor came rushing upstairs. I could have sworn I'd lost my memory and it was really "happening" – very strange.

PS If there is owt you would particularly like me to get for you over in Kirkwall I will do so. Just let me know.

> *Wren Tel L.M.Walker*
> *Haybrake*
> *Lyness*
> *9th March*

My dear Mum and all,

You will be glad to know I came out of sick bay on Wednesday afternoon feeling quite fit. Actually, I should have come out on Thursday, but there is a mild epidemic of gastric flu here, so they sent me out Wednesday. However, my throat is quite clear and better than it has been for a long time.

I was very glad to have your nice letters last night, I also received one from Auntie Ada. Sorry Brenda has been so poorly, I will try to write today. I am going to work for the first time this afternoon.

Mum, if I were you, I would get your teeth from Mr Parkins. Do you want to wait till I come home? If so, I will go with you, but if not, go now. He is very good, though expensive, but I know he will make a good job of them.

Yesterday was our day off (it was mine in any case). I told you we had planned to go to Rackwick. Well, we didn't start out very early, in fact, it was 3pm. Five of us went. We got a hitch in an army lorry for about seven miles and thought we might get a lift the other seven to Rackwick but lifts on that road are few and far between, so we set out to walk. None of us had ever been as far round the coast and it was really beautiful. The road there runs on top of the cliffs and on one side – the left – we had all the hills and on the right and indeed three quarters of the way round us, an unending stretch of sparkling sea and islands. It was marvellous. As we walked on, we came to the largest hill of the island on the left, which looked, from where we were in the valley, a veritable sheer mountain, and in the little strip of land between the sea and the hills were spread out little crofts, small farms and green fertile land, which seems to comprise the hamlet of Hoy, which lies opposite the island of Pomona (the main island) and where we could see the town of Stromness just across the sea. Down by the seashore, we could see a small farm, a man was ploughing and we could see a few chickens, so Mary Macdonald, who is going on leave on Sunday and who is now hastily collecting eggs (as we shall be doing in a fortnight's time) said, "I wonder if they would be able to sell me some eggs?" We all tripped down to this neat little farmhouse and the door was opened by the sweetest old girl who said she would sell us eggs and asked us all into the kitchen. She and her daughter were typical islanders and very very nice. They gave us tea, delicious hot pasty straight from the oven and spiced buns and jam roll. It was lovely and we were very grateful. It was a very isolated spot and five miles to the nearest shop, which they never visited as all their things came on the mail boat from Stromness. When we asked how often they went to Stromness, the daughter said maybe once or twice a _year_ to settle the "accounts". What an isolated existence, but they looked well and were so pleasant. The house was panelled in wood inside and had a peculiar stove where they burned mostly peat, but it was cosy and pretty warm and quite prosperous for the farms out there.

We didn't manage to walk any further because it was after five and looking like rain. We walked back for over an hour and then a lorry overtook us, and we had yet another lift and were back in time for supper, which was egg on toast.

Later, we went to the garrison to see the film "Dragon Seed". We were lucky again and had a lift there and back, so that was the end of a very pleasant day.

Must dry up now.

Much love,

Mary

PS Have you got the film yet?

> Wren Tel L.M.Walker
> Haybrake
> Lyness
> 12/3/45

My dear Mum and all,

So many thanks for the nice letters and snaps received at 2am yesterday. You are getting a pair of giddy young kippers to be sure, going to the pictures so often and sitting on the back row of all things, starting to hold hands again, what? Still, seriously, I <u>am</u> glad you are feeling brighter. Mum, what with your new teeth and new corsets and picturing I shall expect you to look <u>almost</u> as young as Dad, who is now I should think about twenty-five!!!

There is little new since I wrote you last to tell you about our trip. I am feeling okay now and looking forward to seeing you all very soon. I do hope you will be able to get a film for the camera. Glad to hear Brenda is a little better, I still haven't written to them yet, but I do seem to be terribly busy, but <u>will</u> try and write today.

I was going to suggest we try to buy some cutlery for Pat, but Betty and Flo and I have bought her a present now. For a long time, she has wanted one – a model destroyer made by one of the men up here. It is awfully nice and a perfect little model about two feet long and she wants to keep it as a souvenir of Scapa days and is going to name it after one of the destroyers, so I think it's quite a good idea. I _did_ think of buying something for Dorothy whose birthday (wedding???) comes off very soon – what do you suggest??

Do you remember my telling you about some of the girls being ill? There are quite a few more ill now and they are not allowed to have visitors yet and apparently it is not merely gastric flu but, according to rumour, a form of dysentery and exhaustive tests of the water, etc., are being made and attempts made to avoid any more spreading of the epidemic, which is rather disturbing.

I think that will have to be all for the moment.

Lots of love,

Mary

PS Let me know if you want anything bringing when I come.

Sorry I'll not be able to bring any sweets this time, but we only have two bars a week about and we have to share them so much and these days we don't get any from the canteen. I'm terribly sorry because I do like to bring you things!!

15

Spring

A few sunny calm days, warm, the weather website announces high pressure. Misty mornings, the hills veiled in a skin of low cloud. One bright morning (the 13th of March), the pied wagtails are back, swooping and whooping round the house, returned from wherever they spent the winter. It's good to have them around again, bobbing on the wall.

With a friend's company, I start to feel better, enough even to go out every night: a poetry reading, book group, meal with friends, a film, and another meal. You could be out every night being sociable in Orkney if you wanted.

The old Rayburn stove, removed from the kitchen when the new heating system was installed, has been sitting in the garage all winter as I'd failed so far to find a home for it. I tried again, posting it for sale on Orkney Merkit Place, the Facebook page to go to when you want to buy or sell anything. There was plenty of interest, and I had a virtual queue lined up to come and get it. The nice thing about the Merkit Place is that you can see people telling their mates about a post, or conferring as to the usefulness of something. Comments like: Allan Clouston, for your shed? Or Jamie Spence, would this do for my still? (Still!!!) In the end, after a couple of mind changers who'd wanted to re-convert it back to solid fuel until they found out the cost of that, it was Big J who came up trumps.

A muffled and crackly phone call or two from the isle of Hoy had warned me that when a shadow fell across the sun and the doorway filled up, that would be Big J arriving. He was coming from Hoy the morn and would be arriving by t★★★(white noise) around 9.30am because the friend who'd promised him a lift had let him down. I'd assumed the t★★★ was a taxi, but no, he turned up, blocking the sun in the doorway, by t★★★★★★= tractor. Big J lived up to his name and stepped into the house brandishing a tin of biscuits. I showed him the stove, but he was more interested in the garage. "Ooh, self-catering accommodation," he exclaimed, and proceeded to tell me, like others before him, how much I could make if I converted it into rooms. "You could do it on the sly," he told me.

We came to an agreement about the stove. "A pity we can't get it into the trailer today," I remarked, nodding out towards his transport.

"Well, a few years ago, I could have just picked that up by myself," he sighed, "but not now, I've got a bit of back trouble." And he sat down, lit a cigarette and talked. Amongst his other interests he's a pig farmer, and keen to get me involved. I could buy a few piglets, Tamworths they are, and fatten them up, take them to the boar at so-and-so and sell them as in-pig sows. Very friendly they are, very intelligent. And they'd plough my field up in no time. Back in the kitchen, "Do you like winkles?" he asked my friend. Non-plussed at this non-sequitur, N replied in the negative. Big J was undeterred. "The tides are just right for picking them now, you just go out there with a bucket, you can make a bit of money at it." The conversation spooled on, rabbits being the next topic, and he recounted how he and his mate would go out and shoot them or use the ferrets. They'd been invited to go and reduce the rabbit population of North Ronaldsay, but they hit a sticking point: no guns, it'll frighten the breeding birds, and no ferrets – they might escape and eat the breeding birds. "So that was the end of that jaunt," said Big J. "How the hell did they think we were going to catch them, without shooting them or ferrets?"

He went off in the end, in his tractor, promising to send someone to pick up the stove at a later date, and issuing a pressing invitation to visit him on Hoy.

March 21st

Not ever so spring-like, but bright enough and not cold. A pair of ravens glide along the cliff edge between Marwick Head and Birsay Bay. One of them suddenly kinks a sideways twist, wings vertical and streamlined, falls a couple of metres before straightening out again. What's all that about? Evasive action? Showing off? The fulmars are harassing them, but there didn't seem to be any around to trigger that reaction. A bit of research suggests that ravens get together for aerobatic flying just for fun. Amongst the general crow-like squawks they make there's a gentler, quiet sound, like a squeaky wheelbarrow.

From my kitchen window, I watch the *teeos* – lapwings – demonstrating their aerial prowess: flapping, climbing, soaring and diving, and in the back garden, a pair of mallards give a heads up over the tussocky grass. The skylarks are singing again. The curlews have a parabolic flight pattern: flap steeply up into the wind to the top of the curve, soar gently down, and then repeat. Everything is pairing up.

There's a meeting of the Barony Mill steering group, set up as an offshoot of the Birsay Heritage Trust, to deal solely and specifically with the Mill. I feel like a spare part on the committee; amongst the marketing expert, the accountant and the farming contractor, what have I got to offer? I seem to be the only one with any interest in the visitors' side of things. Rae reports on the sales. At the recent Trade Fair, some Chinese women asked him for some oat flakes to send to China. At last, an old friend's prediction has come true: years ago, back in the mists of time when I was a marine biologist, he complained about the rise of Chinese takeaways. What were we doing eating food from the other side of the world? And he wondered if the wee Chinamen are eating porridge over there. Now, apparently, they are, and some of it will have come from Barony Mill, Birsay.

April 7ᵗʰ 2016

The days are suddenly longer, and it really is spring. Celandines appear, marsh marigolds, daffodils, dandelions and scurvy grass are flowering. It's time to get into the garden and one day I decide to tackle the pampas grass; I want to take out the huge clump that's dying from the middle outwards in my oval garden. Perhaps not a good idea for someone convalescing from a nasty virus, but it has to be done. I set to with fork and spade and, sure enough, the dead clumps came up easily. Then an idea struck – how about a fire? It went up really well. *Really* well. The fuschia bush was a bit near, a few neighbouring plants were scorched, and now I'm left with ugly blackened stumps of tussocks, and I had a relapse. Is this what it's like, getting old: taking ages to recover from an infection? Not having enough energy to do the garden?

★ ★ ★

Returning at midnight from a trip Sooth I was astonished to look out of the back window the next morning to see that my back garden appeared to have been newly ploughed, matching the field next door in its blackness. On closer inspection, with eyes properly open, I realised it wasn't ploughed but *burned*. Rae had been threatening to bring his flamethrower for some time and had taken advantage of my absence to do a bit of fire-raising. Somewhat disconcerting, as I'd imagined he only meant to burn the piles of cut grass. But it would grow.

Sure enough, after a couple of weeks, and some rain to

dissipate the burning smell, the new growth was attracting the hares. There were three of them frequenting my patch, nibbling enthusiastically at the juicy dandelions and other luscious young shoots. I watched them for hours. Hares can often be seen in threes at this time of the year: a male will 'guard' a fertile female, staying close to her and chasing off a rival male. One of them would twitch an ear, which alerted me to its presence, nipping off shoots or digging at roots, and then a flurry of activity might reveal two more hares. The rival would gradually, with apparent sly nonchalance, hop nearer to the female until the guarding male could stand it no more and chase the intruder off. They must be the most camouflaged of all the mammalian inhabitants, especially now I have the black burnt bit, which help the black tips to the ears and base of the hare's tail to blend in. The nap of the fur mirrors the lie of the grasses and the match between the bleached straw colours of the vegetation and the under parts is near perfect. Amazingly, I learn that hares only suckle their young for three minutes a day. Three minutes!! The three or four leverets disperse a few days after birth, lying low during the day. Somehow, once a day after sunset, they gather together where they were born and meet up with Mum for a quick guzzle before splitting up again. It doesn't always work; not only do they sometimes choose the wrong mother (who does usually feed them) but they might even hopefully follow a lamb or lapwing, who isn't so obliging.[23]

After a couple of days, the group of three has reduced to two. I guess the rival male has finally been seen off. The pair

23 *The Brown Hare*, Stephen Tapper. Pub. The Mammal Society, 2010.

spend the morning feeding close together in my back garden. They lollop off into the ploughed field and one of them has a cat-like, back-rubbing roll around before snuggling down into the earth quite out of sight. Next morning, I look out to see a gull in the next field, looking guilty. It tugs at something, and I see the black-tipped ears, the sandy coloured belly. Oh no! It must be one of 'my' hares! The male, or the female, or the rival? I can't even be sure that it's nature (red in tooth and claw) because it could be an accident (speeding bloody car). But over the following days, there are once more two hares around; I just don't know which ones they were.

It's quite strange having the light evenings again. Unsettling. And I can't remember what I used to do in the evenings last year. It seems like cheating to read a book when it's bright outside. No doubt I'll get used to it, but some days there's a gnawing sense of loss, of longing. Prowling from room to room, shifting and fidgeting, I gaze out at the light – the colours of fields and sky. Instinctively, almost, I have an urge to drink a glass of wine, or smoke a cigarette, despite having given up the latter thirty years ago, and almost given up the former. The melancholy of the long, light nights. What is it that's missing, what do I lack that would make me fulfilled and complete? There's more to it than lack of a partner. Is it a sense of home, or companionship, or being in the place? I have boxes of pebbles and shells collected over a lifetime, stored for years at my parents' house, my original home in Sheffield. The boxes moved with me to another home, where my son grew up, but they never got unpacked. There was always a feeling that it was temporary, and I would unpack them, distribute them in the garden, when I found my place. I brought them here to Orkney, convinced that this would be their final destination, yet there they are, still in the boxes and basins in the garage. What am I waiting for?

It's not that I've never been settled, there have been many moments of contentment, feeling that this is it, I'm here. But it never lasted. Something always kept driving me on. In older age, it can't be the urge to find a mate and breed; I've already done that. So, what *am* I looking for?

Some people I know are renting a house in Kirkwall. They've moved from the south of England and are here for a one-year trial period. After that, they'll decide whether to stay or go back home. As I reach my first anniversary of moving here, I'm asking myself: what if I'd done that – would I want to go back to my old house, or would I stay here? Myself is deafeningly silent. Neither of us knows the answer to that one.

Wren Tel L.M.Walker
Haybrake
Lyness
22nd April 1945

My dear Mum and all,

Hello you, with your glorious spring weather! We have actually had <u>snow</u> here, and there is quite a covering in the hills. I do hope you haven't had any to ruin the fruit.

We have had one day, however, that was really lovely. I will tell you about it. On Wednesday, we set out from Lyness at 10.30 on a gloriously sunny morning with a chilly sea breeze blowing, and sailed in a small drifter to Houton, a minute little hamlet at the foot of a steep hill and about six miles from Stromness. From there, we went in an army lorry to Stromness. I have never been there before, and it is one of the loveliest places I have ever been. It is much more quaint and old-fashioned than Kirkwall and is utterly unspoilt. It is built on the hillside and is full of unexpected steps and tiny narrow streets and queer old grey stone houses and nearly every house had a bright brass doorknocker. The sea comes up to the backs of the houses on the main street and reminded me of Cornwall, except that the Cornish villages have to a great extent been spoilt by the boom in trippers, whereas this place is so genuine.

By the time we arrived, we were feeling rather chilled and so set about finding a place to eat. We understood this might be a difficult job. However, we found a little place where we thought we could get a cup of tea. When I told the woman we were from Lyness, she said, "Come into the dining room and have a warm by the fire. I expect you'd like some bacon and eggs." Naturally, we didn't say no and had a delicious meal of ham and egg and lovely bread and rolls and butter and oatcakes and all kinds of tarts. It was, indeed, a pleasant surprise.

After exploring the town a bit, and endeavouring to do some shopping, we started walking in the direction of – as we thought – Birsay. After a couple of miles, we discovered that we were on the wrong road. We didn't mind because it was such a perfect day, and all the islands were lovely amid the shimmering vivid blue of the sea. From where we were, we could see the northernmost part of our island (Hoy) where the cliffs are the highest in Britain, and we could see the coast of Scotland.

Turning back to our original destination, we hitched a lift on a lorry on the Kirkwall road, and due to a misunderstanding, he dropped us off at the wrong corner, so we gave up hope of getting to Birsay and decided to continue on the way to Kirkwall.

Between Stromness and Kirkwall, there are lovely lochs here and there. We thought at first it was the sea, they are so much alike. Along the road, there were masses of primroses, and the fields were brilliant with them. We, of course, picked huge bunches and sauntered on in the glorious sunshine, watching wee lambs not more than three or four days old. We stopped and sat on a wall by an old farm, prosperous looking and old with a courtyard and battlements and a little wood golden with primroses and celandines, and we watched the Mediterranean blue of the sea just beyond. A little further on, we came to a lovely one-street village called Finstown with its white cottages, ivy and clematis-covered, and the sea lapping gently within a few inches of their back gardens.

We were getting hungry by now and decided to get to Kirkwall promptly. We hitched a lorry and soon arrived at the Wrennery. By this time, we were very tired, so decided to have a poached egg on toast at the canteen and do the first house at the flicks, have an early supper and go to bed. Next morning, we caught the early drifter and went to work at noon.

Well, my old sparrows, that's enough of my doings. Your lovely letters are smashing, I'm so glad you are having such good weather. Dad, the bluebells you mention in the garden are wild hyacinths, of which there are a lot up here, I planted them a couple of years ago.

How is the old car going? Is Uncle Bill still having to push it?

Must go on duty now, so cheerio, my old ducks.
Love,
Mary xxx

Same old joint
2nd May

My dear Mum and all,
I've put the 2nd of May at the top of this letter but it's actually only the 1st but will be 2nd before I've finished it. Before I forget, Mum, when you send my shirt, will you also send the following:

1 white linen blouse
1 pair elastic laces
2 tins peanut butter
2 vests
Thanks very much.

How are you getting on with your spring-cleaning? Hope you haven't been overdoing it, Mum, whitewashing, etc. – don't forget that rest. We really <u>will</u> do that business about my getting your meals ready next time <u>and</u> no interruptions.

It's been beastly cold here but is slightly better than it has been. Sunday was fearfully cold, and we had to go to bed early to keep warm and we had snow in the air, but it did not stay except on the hills.

Yesterday was our communications club dance and we had a very good evening, even though my partner for the evening turned out to be a stoker.

After all this time, we have at last been out to tea at the house of the officer I told you about. I phoned up last week and arranged to go. Betty went with me, and we had an awfully nice time. They are a very sweet couple, and the little boy is such a bright kid, though rather lonely, he'd suit Brenda as a pal. They live in a small hut, very small to see it from the outside but awfully comfortable inside, and with two bedrooms and a bathroom. Their home is at Minehead, and JW was actually born at Nether Stowey, isn't it strange? He knew the place where we stayed – Appletree Cottage – quite well. We came back having thoroughly enjoyed the afternoon. JW came in and had tea with us. I wonder what some of the girls would have said if they'd seen us! Anyhow, it was very pleasant, and I hope to go again before very long.

Have just had a letter and stamps from Friday night class. I do hope Dad's cold is better – if the weather has been anything like the weather here, I'm not surprised at anyone having colds.

Can't think of anything more, so will finish just before midnight.
Lots of love to all of you,
Mary

PS Have just received your letter, many thanks, sorry about the parcel, but as a matter of fact I didn't take it to be censored myself, but I've told you the conditions before and all the things were there anyhow, ducks – it was quite securely packed. What I want to know is: did you like the skirt? And does it fit? Please tell me!

16

VE Day

Haybrake
Lyness
Orkney
8ᵗʰ May 1945

My dear Mum and all,

Well! Today is the day we have been waiting for for so long and, strangely enough, there's quite a flat feeling in the air – no excitement, just like an ordinary day. Perhaps down the line things will be different. We were off duty when we heard the news; as a matter of fact, I was just coming out of the bath and the others were nearly all asleep. A little later, we went out to the canteen, Betty and I, and had a coffee and poor old Betty was terribly upset. She is usually so placid, but she wept for a long time. Of course, both her brothers are away and her other brother was killed (or died, rather) as a result of the war, her Auntie too was drowned when the Athenia was sunk and she has lost a lot of friends who were pals of her brother who have been killed, so you can imagine she was thinking about them. To finish matters, she had a letter from her mother telling her that her grandmother died on Saturday; she was about eighty-six and had been ill for a long time. The funeral is today, so you will realise that Mrs B will not feel in a very joyful mood. We could not go to church being on duty – now I am writing this just before Mr Churchill's speech.

Up here, we cannot relax for quite a while because there are still U-boats to be accounted for and you cannot trust them one iota, as you know, and there may be many who still haven't heard the news.

Tonight, we are having a party with big eats, and I imagine great crowds. I would like to be at home, though, and see the bonfire up at Slayleigh. Quite soon, at 3pm, you will be listening to Mr Churchill, me too, as I think will everyone else in these isles.

I was so glad to hear from you last night. I do hope your cold is better, Mum. I wonder if Dorothy will get her hair done today, isn't it funny, just making the appointment for today?

That's all for now,

Cheerio – lots of love, Mary

Wren Tel L.M. Walker
Haybrake
Lyness
11ᵗʰ May

My dear Mum and all,

I began to write to you yesterday morning, but I had so many interruptions that I had to scrap it. First of all, Uncle Bill, thanks very much indeed for the ten bob. It was great because I was absolutely stony having put £2 in the PO since I came back, and I didn't want to draw any out because it never goes back, and I had just 3/- to last nearly a fortnight, so it just came at the right moment.

My last letter was written just before Mr Churchill spoke, if I remember rightly; we heard him speak as we sat on watch. Everyone heard it as all the sets were quite quiet. Immediately afterward, the signal came through over the air and we had to send it out to all the ships: "Splice the mainbrace".[24] Unfortunately, we couldn't, but the men all did it quite thoroughly.

At supper time, it was a sort of "help yourself" meal with Spam and tongue and cheese, jam, etc., etc., to which we all did full justice, and it was good in spite of the Admiralty order that on VE day there were to be "No repetition, No special meals".

Later in the evening, there was a very crowded dance, during which we all very solemnly listened to the King's Speech and sang the King at midnight or rather 0001, all the hooters and sirens of all the ships went (as had happened at the end of Mr Churchill's speech), they made a terrific racket. Very lights[25] and rockets were fired and altogether it was rather unforgettable. It was a pity it was such a filthy day – in London it was apparently glorious weather.

The next morning, we were on duty at 0800 and were pretty tired. I had the first watch off, fortunately, so was able to go out in the evening. Betty was unlucky, however, and had to go on duty. I went out to a dance on the Flagship; in the afternoon, the weather had been pretty foul, but it was a glorious evening, and the sun was quite warm. An awning had been put over the part of the deck where the dance was to be held and there were even heaters on deck; altogether, it was very well done. As usual, we met "sparkers" (wireless operators) and went round the ship chiefly to the W/T office. However, it was terribly interesting, and I had never been on board before and always wanted to go. They had coloured lights all the way round the dance space and

---

24 'Splice the mainbrace' was the order given to issue celebratory tots of rum.

25 Very lights were flares, coloured or white, invented by an American, Edward W. Very, and were fired from pistols for signalling.

there was a space allowed below decks in case the weather was too bad, and plenty of big eats too. It was rather unfortunate that my escort was not just the one I wanted and, unfortunately, I could not dispose of him very easily. It was also a pity that another fellow that I know and like was there alone, and I couldn't do anything about it. Also, one of my old "pashes" – an officer whom I had once arranged to meet and accidentally didn't – was there with someone I knew. Still, it was quite a good evening otherwise, and everybody had a super time. When it came to 10.30 and time to go, many of the fellows crowded on deck to wave goodbye and we all cheered and sang as the little boat packed with Wrens glided away from the great ship. We waved until we were out of sight and sang all the way back; indeed, you would have thought we were quite mad or at least very tight, but we were all just happy, it had been such a successful evening.

All the way up from the pier to the Wrennery, I have never seen anything like it, we were just crazy, singing and dancing around and every poor little matelot who came down, we danced around him and shrieked madly, but it was great fun, and everybody seemed to be infected by the spirit of the evening. When in later years anyone says, 'what did you do on VE day?' it will not be difficult to remember.

I was fortunate enough to be able to spend nearly twelve hours in bed afterward and got up just in time to have my hair set. In the evening, we went to the film "The Constant Nymph", which was pretty good. Now we are on the morning watch, and it is about 0400. I shall sleep all day until teatime then Betty and I are going to the Fleet dance at Flotta – we may as well make a week of celebrations.

Now I must become more sober and come back to earth. I was greatly distressed to hear about Sheila Hudson. She had looked, I thought, *very ill when I saw her last and seemed to be rapidly getting thinner and had been off work for a while. Have you phoned Beryl at all, I wonder? Isn't it strange that Madge should die so suddenly and that Sheila, who took her place, died just two years after. What tragedies seem to be happening in our firm, that is the fourth death in a very short time. I should hate to go back, I think I would rather go out scrubbing floors than go back.*

I am so glad your cold is much better, Mum, do try and keep resting. Everybody is having two days' extra leave – I only hope it is still on when I come home, then I shall be home for my birthday.

Did Dorothy get her perm? I had a letter from Mrs Dodgson and from Brenda, I am glad they are going away again.

Sorry Chrissie is going away, but I don't think it will be as long as three years, it should only be two, and will be over maybe even quicker.

Now I'll leave you, so for now cheerio and tons of love,

Mary

PS Thanks awfully, Mum, for offering to dye my shirt and collar, I should be glad if you would.

Haybrake
Lyness
12th May 45

My dear Mum and all,

I was so thrilled to get your lovely long letter, you sounded much better and more like yourself; I can always tell from your letters just how you are, they are a great indication of how you feel. I'm so glad you enjoyed VE day, yes, we will have our day when I come home. Up here, we are speculating how long it will be before we are home. Yes, we are getting the extra two days as you thought, so all being well, I should be home for my birthday.

To suggest that your letter would bore me is absolute tripe, I love to hear from you, and you always tell me just the things I want to hear.

Your news regarding Kathy left me speechless, whatever must Charlie have felt like when he came home to such a situation? The awful thing is that he hasn't a home himself. I really cannot find adequate words to express my feelings about such people; it has just happened at the wrong moment for her. I can imagine how upset Auntie Ada will be, fancy them never telling her until she really <u>had</u> to know. You'll probably have heard more news next time you write, do let me know all about it. (Sorry for having to continue in pencil.)

I now begin in ink again (Sunday forenoon).

Many thanks for the laces and elastic. The envelope was split up the side, it's much the elastic hadn't come out, but it was okay. I would have loved to have seen you looking glamorous on VE day, Mum, and what's this about your hair? Have you had it permed yet? I do wish you would, old girl. Wasn't it nice of Mrs J to do Dorothy's?

If it is at all possible, Mum, to put in a small tin of any sort of jam when you send the peanut butter, I shall be very glad. You see, I have so much of Betty's, and I did not bring any back with me, it will do any time. I think the only place where you can buy the peanut butter is on Chapel Walk, but don't go out specially for it, any time you are passing will do.

I went over to Flotta to a ship's dance. It wasn't so good as some we have been to; the best part of the evening was when we came back. As we went down to the little old stone jetty, we looked out to sea, it was as flat and calm and still as the pond opposite our house with scarcely the merest ripple. The sunset was just in its earliest stages and the reflection in the water was the palest gold, gradually changing to pink as we sailed along. We seemed to just drift along through the flat pool which was the sea. The hills looked black against the glorious evening sky, and the wide expanse of the Flow with the lovely, graceful ships at anchor was utterly unmarred by anything ugly – an altogether peaceful picture. We waved as we passed tugs and destroyers, trawlers and drifters and the numerous little craft on their way to and from the harbour.

Yesterday was a lovely sunny day, but I had the afternoon watch and could not go out, but this afternoon we are hoping to go on another ship, one which we always hoped to go on last year and never had an opportunity. There is a special thanksgiving service on board the flagship today, I would have liked to have gone, but duty called.

Now I'll have to do some work,
    Much love,
    Mary

Haybrake
Lyness
17/5/45

My dear Mum and all,

Just a very wee note this time because I'm awfully rushed. Very very many thanks for your nice letters – I was so pleased with your news that Mum had actually been out twice on Sunday and had her hair permed, things are looking up – and it must look nice if you say so, Dad.

Thanks for the lining, I shan't bother having it re-lined, I'm hoping I shan't want it very much longer. Glad you enjoyed the services, I wish

I had been with you. Thanks for the papers, it was nice to read about the happenings at home on VE day. There are wild rumours here about what is going to happen to us, and they are different every day, but what I do know is I'm going to keep my eyes open for the sort of job I want. If you hear of any plans for training people in the sort of work I want to do please find out and let me know.

Today, Betty, Mary and I went out cycling for a wee while and did enjoy it. It was a lovely afternoon and glorious sailing along by the sea; the hills, the sea and everything was wonderful, even climbing the hills we didn't mind. We wore civvies and felt really free and full of beans. Now I feel a wee bit stiff round the rear end. After we got back, we went to see the film "Frenchman's Creek". Last night, after we came off the last Dog, we went to see the film "Arsenic and Old Lace". It is really very funny and we both enjoyed it thoroughly.

So sorry to hear Monty is dead, poor wee thing. We have a little dog here very much like him, only younger.

Betty is glad to hear you are becoming a good Scot – a _wee_ bit of toffee indeed!! I haven't received the parcel yet but expect to have it by tomorrow am.

That's all for now.

Lots of love.

Mary

PS I did not send the photo to Hilda as none of the ones I had left were any good, but sent a letter and a card. Edith liked her hanky, I heard from her yesterday.

PPS Parcel just arrived – many many thanks.

Mary

Haybrake
Lyness
20th May 45

My dear Mum and all,

It was nice to talk to you last night. I'm afraid I was rather incoherent, but I expect you got the general idea.

I am going on draft on Thursday, so don't write to me again here. I am going to Drem, a naval air station about half an hour south of Edinburgh. It'll be a bit of a nuisance leaving because I do like it here, but we are all going, so it can't be helped. There are nine Wrens, two leading Wrens and one PO going, and Betty is going, of course, so it won't be so bad. Another of our friends went on draft yesterday and we all seem to be splitting up. Flo is going too, so are Betty Williamson and Rose, but they volunteered; there weren't enough volunteers, so they drew out of the hat and we came out too. However, it might be worse, and I shall be much nearer home – only six hours away, so I'll be able to come home when I get a weekend off – good oh! And I shall be able to go to Edinburgh with Betty. I will try and get the tweed tomorrow. All this has come rather suddenly, so there is a lot of confusion up here. I shall send my civvies on to Mrs Burnett's, so I shall not have very much to carry. Today all the staff of Wee Fea have had their photographs taken, rather sad in a way, still it was inevitable with the European war at an end.

I will write again later in the week. Thanks, Mum, for your lovely letter full of news and thanks too for the welcome stamps.

That's all for now, am just going to church.

Love,
Mary

171

17

Postscript

Wren Tel L. M. Walker 94167
WRNS Quarters
Drem
East Lothian
Scotland
26ᵗʰ May 45

My dear Mum and all,

We arrived here yesterday morning, just before noon, and we are feeling rather like fish out of water being on land, so to speak, once more. The journey was not too bad; we had quite a long time to wait in Thurso, so whiled away the time as usual by having a meal.

I have not written you a decent letter since goodness knows when, so scarcely know where to begin. First of all I will tell you about the tweed. I received the wired £6 on Monday and Betty received hers at the same time, many thanks for getting it off so promptly. When we arrived in Kirkwall, we went straight to the tweed shop and, to our dismay (for Betty and I both wanted the same kind of material), we discovered they had none of the nice navy tweed, which we had seen before, but only the brown, which I have sent, and some horrid check material. We were so disappointed, but I think that it would quite suit you, Mum, but if you think definitely not then we will either sell it or

I may decide to keep it for myself, so I have not spent any coupons yet. However, if you definitely don't like it, Mum, I will see what I can do here in Edinburgh. Betty has sent her mum the same material, but we have not heard her reactions yet – she is going to try to persuade her to keep it.

When we arrived in Edinburgh, we thought we would have plenty of time to go to Betty's, however we only had just over an hour, but it is only about five mins from the station, so we were okay. Mr Burnett met us because her mum had to go to her auntie's early in the morning, so her dad stayed off working till just after 9am and cooked us porridge and we had a nice breakfast by the fire. Betty was looking forward to our going so near Edinburgh, naturally, as we are just like Dronfield is to Sheffield, but I said I did not want to go every time and "put upon" them sort of business. Well, of course, Betty told her dad all this and he said I was to go like going home, etc., etc., etc., and wouldn't hear of me going anywhere else and I would always be welcome, etc., etc., etc., so that was okay. So, we had breakfast and then left on the 10.40 train and arrived at Drem in just over thirty minutes.

(I'm finishing this at Mrs Burnett's, Saturday afternoon. We are out until midnight but I've a feeling I shan't be able to finish this because it's not awfu' quiet, as you may imagine. However, if you'll just regard this as the first instalment, I'll finish it tomorrow afternoon when I am off duty. Actually, we seem to have quite a lot of time off and rather a cushy job working, of course, with planes and not with ships.

Now I'll leave you and write a really decent letter tomorrow.
Much love,
Mary xxx

PS Mrs Burnett does not like the tweed..

PPS Will be seeing you every eight weeks from now on – what about slipping up to Edinburgh for a holiday? We get a sleeping out pass every week!!!!!!

And so, things came to an end. The war was over, people came back, or they didn't. You'll be wondering what became of my dear mum, who'd so adamantly declared, "I <u>won't</u> go back to work for her (Miss Hensman, chief clerk at BTH) if I have to beg from door to door – I'd rather starve … I'd rather go scrubbing floors." All that talk of looking for the sort of job she really wants, and training opportunities; did she make use of all she learned, all that physics, all that extra confidence and responsibility gained from being away from home? Sadly, no. Reading her letters made my heart ache for that twenty-four-year-old, because I knew she was going to make a decision she would come to regret later, that this enthusiasm and ambition would disappear. How did it happen? Why did she go back to BTH electrical company and take up her old position? What happened to that claim that she'd rather scrub floors?

There were training opportunities, and some of her friends in later life were those who'd taken advantage of them, doing teacher training and progressing in that profession. "I was daft," she said, "I should have done it." She was just as bright, or brighter, just as able as them. Why didn't she do it? Was it a question of money? Mum ended up working as a secretary for a primary school headteacher who'd been one of these, and knew bitterly that she could have done the job just as well.

Years later, she wrote:

Like many of my contemporaries, I vowed I would never go back to my old job but, of course, I did. With hindsight, this was a stupid decision. I rejected the idea of social work and very seriously considered teaching. Indeed, I passed the test with flying colours and was offered a place on a one-year emergency training course at Psalter Lane[26] and turned it down. Still, that's water under the bridge and life went on rather drearily, it must be said, after the excitement of previous years.

I can only guess that she went into a bit of a depression, a sort of culture shock brought on by being back home after the excitement of wartime, the togetherness and camaraderie of life in the cabin, the work at the base. It must have been a bit like that feeling at the end of university, the leaving of friends and going back home and wondering what on earth to do with the rest of your life. When I was going through it, she told me as much in almost so many words. So, even though she passed the test and had a place to do teacher training, she opted for safety, didn't take it up, but went back to her old job with BTH and Miss Hensman, she of the used hanky. She met my dad at a church social for returning service personnel, during which they took part in a charade supposed to represent 'washing an elephant'. Dad was a handsome man and, like Mum, had what they called a 'good' war, stationed in Egypt and Palestine. He was gentle, hard-working, full of humour, didn't like an argument, and as I write this, I hear my mother describing *her* father. So, once the elephant was duly

---

26 Former teacher training college in Sheffield, not far from her home.

cleaned and the game over, he walked her home and they got together. They were married four years later, moved in with her parents – still in the rented house they escaped to after the blitz – and that put an end to any career plans that might have developed as she got her confidence back. She got on with the business of being a wife and mother, looking after her mother and eventually going back to work at part-time jobs she could fit round family life, staying in the same house for the next fifty-two years.

As for me, the result of this stable and secure background seems to be that I continually sought out danger, change and upheaval; although, in terms of a career, I was as lacking in ambition as my mum. But, wherever I wandered, there was always home.

A year after moving to Orkney, I nervously accepted an invitation to visit Sheffield, my 'home place' as my Tanzanian students would call it. It was to be the longest stay for several years. How would it be, this 'home' with these memories and these absences? The last time I approached the city by train was when my son was little, he'd been about four years old, and my parents waited excitedly on the platform, delight spilling out of them as they greeted their only grandchild and only surviving child. The memory didn't hurt; it felt like coming home.

Grief never goes away but accompanies us along our way, close or more distant. It runs to catch us and give a nudge, or leaps forward to trip us up when we're least expecting it.

It might pop up in the night to wake me from a dream and I lie there, feeling that I was never in the right place at the right time, or never in the right place long enough. Feeling that I could have done better. You do the best you can when there's nobody to tell you what to do.

In Sheffield, I felt shockingly at home. One day, I went to Shepherd's Wheel, an abandoned water mill where I used to play as a child. Now it's been restored and works at weekends. My oldest friends Gina and Bob explain the history to visitors, the story of how, in the early days of Sheffield cutlery, knives were ground in the mills in the valleys.

"Are you from Sheffield?" Gina asked a woman.

"Oh yes," says the visitor confidently, and then hesitates. "Well… I've been here twenty-six years, so…" she tails off, with a little laugh.

Overhearing, my body is outraged. It's a physical reaction. How can she say she's *from* Sheffield? *I'm from* Sheffield! Whether I live here or not.

In Orkney they have a good way round this.

"Do you stay in Orkney?" they'll ask you. By *stay* they mean live – do you live here? So, I can say confidently yes, I do stay here. I don't need to add 'but I'm not *from* here'; everyone can tell that by my voice. Even if I stay here for thirty years, I'll never be from here, and that's fine. I'll never be Orcadian.

Like that migratory bird, however, I've touched down and settled here at the moment and found a niche. Perhaps I'll be here a while. Adventure is still calling, but with a less demanding voice.

Getting up from the desk, I'm drawn as ever to the window; there are ravens on the wall. The tea towel windsock is flapping from the southwest, but it's not too bad. I won't have to lean too far into the wind.

Pulling on boots and coat, I head out to the coast.

Acknowledgements

Thanks to my neighbours in Orkney for making me, a 'ferry-looper', feel so welcome: to Moira and the late Jackie, Billy and Norma, Rena and Juicy. To all at Barony Mill, especially Margaret and her late husband Rae. Thanks to all my friends in Orkney Ramblers and the Scottish Country Dancing group, a more recent addition to my activities. And to old friends, far and wide, without whom this book would never have been published, in particular those who I first dared to show it to – Lesley, Gina and Joanna, thanks for being so encouraging, and to Anne, who helped me to move here.

Many thanks to Jen Parker of Fuzzy Flamingo for her enthusiasm in editing and designing the book, and helping me publish it.

I'm thankful beyond words that my maternal grandmother saved Mum's letters, for without them this book would not have existed. Belated and posthumous thanks to my parents, Mary and Ron, for a childhood in which I felt loved and happy, and for always loving me, whatever. Finally, thanks to my son for being a wonderful, warm, funny human being.